Passionate Poison

Beyond Lust Lies Salvation

By
Linine Langley

Linine Langley

Copyright © 2025 Linine Langley

No part of this publication may be reproduced, stored in a retrieval system, or transmitted in any form or by any means, electronic, mechanical, photocopying, recording or otherwise, without the prior written permission of the copyright owner, except for brief quotations used in reviews or academic work.

Table of Content

Chapter One: House on the Hill 7
Chapter Two: What Next 22
Chapter Three: The Trip 38
Chapter Four: Passionate Poison: Is It More? 50
Chapter Five: The Room 59
Chapter Six: Cracks in The Illusion 70
Chapter Seven: I Have Lost All Trust 85
Chapter Eight: The Hard Way 97
Chapter Nine: Three Can Play the Game 110
Chapter Ten: Beyond Lust Lies Salvation 121
Epilogue: The End of a Reign 133

Linine Langley

This is the most erotic time of my life, an adventure I could never have imagined. I had no idea it would ever lead to this or how things were about to change. How this man was about to change the way I think, the things I do, the lengths I would go to for him and no other. I never imagined I would fall deeply in love with this man and be there for him no matter what. The thought of being hurt had crossed my mind on many occasions, as we never really know anyone fully. We all like to think we do, but in reality, that just doesn't happen. I had to question myself, would I be strong enough to handle it mentally if things went wrong? I don't know the answer to that, but I am willing to take a gamble on it. Sometimes we have to take a chance and not worry about the ifs and buts; life is far too short not to be happy. Enjoy each other while you can.

Passionate Poison

Make Me Your Fantasy
Take Me To Another World

Do we dare act upon our wildest fantasies, or do we just go on in life playing it safe, wondering what if I did do it, what would the outcome have been? Could you live with your decision, and could you just walk away if sex was all it was ever going to be and nothing more? Can you tell the difference between lust and love? Can you tell if you are being conned by the charm of your seducer?

Passionate Poison

Chapter One: House on the Hill

"Flight 567 ready for boarding."

The voice echoes through the terminal, bringing me back out of my daze. I look down at the ticket, Brisbane, seat 14A, and I just sit there staring at it, as if the thing is written with some secret code as to where I need to go next.

Six weeks in Cairns, and I still have no clue.

It was to be a break, time to reflect, time to heal, time to figure out who I am without the name of another person stuck onto the end of mine. But it's been a blur of long walks, too much wine, and far too many self-help paperbacks that all tell the same story: *let go*. It's easy enough to say.

I gather up my belongings and get in the boarding line. Everyone around me is chatting freely, couples chuckling, families shepherding youngsters, businessman typing on their phones. I am standing there, not wanting to be the only individual on the face of the earth who doesn't really fit in anyplace.

Two marriages behind me, a stalled career, and a heart that still can't decide what the hell it wants, not exactly the beacon of success. I'm a master of keeping patient, though. Smile, nod, act like everything's okay.

The thing is, I'm tired. Not just tired of love that went bad, but tired of the continuous striving, striving to be enough, fix things, make people happy. It's as if I've lived all these years constructing sand castles, just watching them get swept away as soon as the tide came in.

Perhaps this flight is not just bringing me home. Perhaps it is bringing me back somewhere I've been a long time, *back home to me*.

I sit down and jam the bag under the one ahead. It smells slightly of coffee and reused air. It's reassuringly quiet, the engine hum comforting. For the first time all week, I have nowhere I must be.

Linine Langley

As the last passengers make their way down the aisle, a man settles into the seat next to me. He looks to be in his mid-forties, relaxed, with sun-kissed skin and an easy grin, suggesting he knows how to go with the flow. He nods in greeting, and I give a polite smile.

The plane starts to taxi, and I grip the armrest a little too tightly. I've never been a good flyer; something about being trapped in a metal tube thousands of feet above the ground doesn't help my nerves. I close my eyes, take a deep breath, and try to focus on the steady hum of the engines.

Then I feel something solid under my hand. Warm. Firm.

I open my eyes.

Oh no.

My hand is on his leg. Not near it. Not brushing against it. No, I'm gripping the man's thigh like it's a lifeline in a storm.

He raises an eyebrow, amusement flashing in his eyes. "Everything alright there?"

I freeze. "Oh God, I'm so sorry! I... I'm terrified of take-offs, and I didn't realise I was,"

"Assaulting my leg?" he finishes, laughing.

I groan, covering my face. "I'll buy you a drink to make up for it. Coffee? Bourbon? A new pair of trousers?"

He chuckles. "Coffee will be fine. I'm Joe, by the way."

"Jane," I reply, still embarrassed. "And thanks for being so understanding about my accidental... assault."

"Well, Jane, if you grab anyone else's leg, make sure they're at least this understanding," he teases, raising his cup in a mock toast.

I laugh, feeling the tension ease. It feels nice to laugh at myself and to remember that not everything has to be serious. We chat briefly about the weather, travel, and how flying brings out the worst in people, but mostly, we sit in comfortable silence.

Passionate Poison

For the first time in months, I don't feel the need to fill every silence with words. Maybe healing doesn't always come from big realisations or perfect endings. Maybe it's found in moments like this, small, silly, human.

As the flight smooths out, I look out the window. The clouds stretch endlessly below, soft and white, like a clean slate. I imagine leaving all the pain and noise down there, floating away until it's too far to touch me anymore.

Two failed marriages. It still stings to say it out loud.

The first one ended quietly, with a slow drifting apart. We became polite strangers sharing a house but not a heartbeat. The second one… well, that was messier. Lies, broken promises, and heartbreak that made me question everything I thought I knew about love.

After that, I promised myself never again. Never to fall or trust completely that I'd lose myself in someone else's shadow.

But sitting here, thousands of feet above the earth, I can admit something I haven't dared say before: I'm tired of being afraid.

Maybe it's time to stop living in reaction to what went wrong. Maybe it's time to start creating what might go right.

The captain's voice comes over the speaker, announcing our descent into Brisbane. My stomach flutters, part nerves, part anticipation.

As the plane dips through the clouds, the city unfolds below. It feels familiar yet distant, shimmering in the afternoon light. Home. Or something like it.

When we land, there's the usual shuffle of passengers reaching for bags, eager to escape. Joe offers to get my suitcase from the overhead compartment, and I thank him with a smile.

"Take care of that hand," he says with a wink. "You never know whose leg it'll find next."

I laugh again, and for the first time in a long while, it feels genuine.

Linine Langley

Outside the airport, the warm air hits me. It's heavy with the scent of rain on hot concrete. The sky is a soft blue-grey, the kind that makes everything look freshly washed. I breathe it in and feel something inside me shift.

I'm home, but I'm not the same woman who left.

I've spent so long trying to be everything, a good wife, a dependable friend, a reliable professional. But who was I when no one was watching?

I don't have the answer yet, but I know this much: it's time to find out.

The taxi driver loads my bag into the boot, and we head toward the city. As the skyline slips into rolling suburbs, I watch the world slide by, jacarandas blooming, kids on bikes, the lazy shimmer of heat off the pavement. Life, ordinary and unbothered, goes on without me.

By the time we pull up at my place, the sun is low, streaking the sky in shades of orange and rose. I pay the driver, drag my suitcase inside, and pause at the door.

It feels strange standing here again, surrounded by the silence that used to feel comforting but now feels like possibility.

I drop my bag, pour a glass of wine, and run a hot bath. As the water fills, I light a candle, something small, just enough to push back the shadows.

Steam curls around me as I sink into the tub. My reflection in the flickering light looks softer somehow, less certain but more alive.

This is where it starts, I tell myself.

No more waiting for permission. No more hiding behind what-ifs.

The past has had its time, all the heartbreak, all the lessons, all the tears. I've carried it long enough.

Tonight, I let it go.

When I close my eyes, I picture the house I saw advertised in the paper earlier, a caretaker position on a property just outside the city, *"The*

Passionate Poison

House on the Hill." It caught my attention for reasons I can't quite explain. Maybe it's the promise of quiet. Maybe it's the sense that something new is waiting there.

Whatever it is, I can feel it, the faint stirring of something that feels a lot like hope.

Tomorrow, I'll call about the job.

Tonight, I'll let the water wash it all away, the fear, the doubt, the ghost of what's been.

And maybe, just maybe, I'll start believing that what lies ahead could be more than just another chapter.

It could be the beginning of a story I finally want to live.

***

The morning light filters through the blinds, soft and golden, nudging me awake. For a moment, I just lie there, listening to the faint hum of the city in the distance: cars, birds, life. It feels good to wake up without that heaviness on my chest.

After a week back in Brisbane, the world already feels a little less uncertain. My things are unpacked, the fridge is stocked, and I've even stopped checking my phone for messages that won't come. That feels like progress.

I make myself a coffee and sit by the window, the newspaper spread out in front of me. The classifieds section is full of options, with half-heartedly circled jobs that I don't really want. Then, in the middle of the page, something catches my eye:

Housemaid Wanted, Private Residence, North Brisbane Hills. Live-in position. Discretion and attention to detail essential.

There's no photo, just an address and a brief description: large heritage property, maintained for professional residence.

I read it twice, then a third time. There's something about it, the simplicity, the mystery. A clean slate, quite literally.

Linine Langley

A live-in job would mean a total break from my old patterns. No clutter of memories, no late-night distractions, no ghosts of what went wrong. Just work, quiet, and maybe the kind of solitude that heals.

Before I can talk myself out of it, I circle the ad, tear it from the paper, and open my laptop. The application form is simple enough: name, experience, references. I mention my background in hospitality, a stint managing short-term rentals, and my eye for order. I fill in the rest with what feels right: reliable, organised, respectful of privacy.

I hit send before I can second-guess myself.

***

Three days later, I receive an envelope in the mail. My name is written neatly on the front in dark ink. I open it quickly, my heart racing.

Dear Ms. Collins,

Thank you for your application. We would like to invite you for an interview at 10 a.m. on Friday. Address enclosed.

Regards,

N. Hawthorne.

The name sticks in my mind. Hawthorne. It sounds elegant, maybe a bit traditional.

I carefully fold the letter and set it on the table, smiling to myself. An interview. It feels like progress, like life is pushing me forward again.

***

Friday morning arrives clear and warm. I take extra care with my clothes, simple but neat: a light blouse, tailored trousers, and my hair tied back. I aim for professional, not overdressed. First impressions matter.

The taxi winds through the suburbs and then upward, the road curving into the hills. The air changes as we climb; it becomes fresher and quieter, while the city shrinks below. When the house comes into view, I have to catch my breath.

Passionate Poison

It sits high on the slope, framed by tall gum trees and hedges trimmed to perfection. A sweeping drive leads to a sandstone façade, with windows gleaming in the sun. It's beautiful and stately without being showy; the kind of house that seems to hold its breath between moments.

I thank the driver, step out, and smooth my palms against my sides. For a long moment, I just stand there, taking it in. There's something about the place, not intimidating exactly, but expectant. It seems like it has been waiting for something or someone.

The front door opens before I can knock. A woman in her sixties appears. Her silver hair is pinned neatly, and she wears a crisp navy uniform. "Ms. Collins?"

"Yes, that's me."

"Mr. Hawthorne will see you shortly. Please, come in."

The hallway is cool and polished, smelling faintly of cedar and lemon. My shoes click softly on the tiled floor as she leads me through to a sitting room. Light spills in from tall windows, warming everything, leather armchairs, a grand piano, and shelves of books that look well-loved rather than decorative.

"Would you like some water while you wait?"

"Yes, thank you."

She leaves, and I wander to the window, glancing out at the gardens. Everything is in perfect order, trimmed hedges, pale roses climbing the stone walls, and a sweep of green rolling into the distance.

There's calm here, structure, and a kind of beauty that doesn't try too hard.

"Ms. Collins."

The voice comes from behind me, smooth, measured, with a hint of quiet command. I turn. Nate Hawthorne stands in the doorway.

He's not quite what I expected. He appears to be in his early forties, tall, with an ease that comes from knowing exactly who he is. His shirt sleeves are rolled up, showing strong forearms dusted with a faint tan. His clear blue eyes meet mine, and for a heartbeat, the air seems to still.

He smiles, not the kind you practice, but one that feels genuine. "Thank you for coming. Please, have a seat."

I do, hoping my hands aren't as visibly unsteady as they feel.

He sits opposite me, studying me with polite attentiveness. "I've read your application. You've had quite a range of experience."

"Yes," I say. "I've worked in private residences before, mostly managing short-term stays. I enjoy the order of it."

"Order," he repeats, as if testing the word. "That's something we value here."

He asks a few more questions, practical things about schedules, duties, and confidentiality. His tone is even and professional, yet there's a quiet energy beneath it. It feels like he listens not just to my answers, but also to the spaces between them.

When our hands brush as I pass him my references, something flickers, brief, electric, and quickly gone. I feel it anyway.

"So," he says after a pause, glancing down at the papers before meeting my eyes again, "why this job, Ms. Collins? You seem overqualified."

I hesitate, then answer honestly. "I think I'm looking for something simple and grounded. I've spent a long time trying to fix other people's messes. Maybe I just want to take care of a place that stays still."

He studies me for a moment longer than feels strictly necessary, then nods slowly. "That's a good answer."

The silence that follows isn't awkward, more like shared understanding that neither of us wants to name.

At last, he stands. "Thank you, Ms. Collins. We'll be in touch within a few days."

Passionate Poison

I rise too, smoothing my blouse and offering a smile that feels a touch too bright. "Thank you for your time, Mr. Hawthorne."

He walks me to the door. Just before I step outside, he says, "Jane, isn't it?"

"Yes."

His smile deepens slightly. "Welcome back to Brisbane."

The words are ordinary enough, but the way he says them feels warm and deliberate, like he means it. It sends a small flutter through my chest.

Outside, the sunlight feels sharper and the air more alive. As the taxi drives me away, I glance back at the house one last time. Its windows catch the light like watchful eyes.

I should be thinking about the practicalities, references, contracts, pay, but all I can think about is the moment he looked at me, really looked.

It's ridiculous, of course. He's my potential employer and nothing more. Still, there's something about him that lingers, the calm certainty, the quiet gravity.

By the time I reach home, I've almost convinced myself I imagined it. Almost.

I change into comfortable clothes, make another coffee, and sit by the window. The letter from the house lies on the table, still unopened. My gaze drifts toward it again, unbidden.

Maybe this job is just what I need: structure, routine, and the peace of a place far removed from the noise of my past.

Yet, a part of me, the restless, curious part I thought I'd left behind, wonders if that house and the man who runs it will be as simple as they seem.

***

The next morning, the phone rings.

"Ms. Collins?"

"Yes, speaking."

"This is Mr. Hawthorne. If you're still interested, we'd like you to start next week."

For a moment, I can't speak. "Yes," I finally say. "I'd like that very much."

"Good," he replies. "We'll see you Monday morning."

When the line goes dead, I find myself staring at the phone, my heart racing with what feels dangerously like excitement.

The house on the hill is waiting.

For the first time in years, I'm ready to see where the road leads.

***

The first week at the house flies by in a mix of order and quiet discovery. Each morning starts the same way: the soft buzz of cicadas outside, the scent of coffee from the kitchen, and the warm sunlight streaming across the veranda. There's something soothing about the place, a steady rhythm that grounds me while awakening feelings I can't identify.

The house has its own character. It breathes quietly, listens through its walls, and seems to hold memories. Each smooth floorboard and framed photo hints at a life lived with care and intention. Everything is organised. Nothing is out of place.

Then there's Nate.

His presence fills the house, even when he's not there. I notice the faint scent of cedar and soap in the hallway, hear his low voice coming from the study, and catch the distant sound of doors opening and closing. It makes the air feel alive.

I pick up on his routine quickly: he wakes up early, enjoys a long black coffee, takes a quick jog around the property, and is in the office by eight. He works with a quiet focus, his eyes steady and his jaw firm. Yet there are brief, genuine moments when he looks up from his screen, sees me walking by, and a slight smile crosses his face.

Passionate Poison

Those moments are risky.

I can easily convince myself that I'm being friendly and polite. But that smile stays with me, lingering at the edges of my thoughts long after I've left the room.

***

By the second week, we had settled into a steady rhythm of quiet conversation and professional ease. I took care of household tasks, ordering supplies, tidying up, and keeping everything running smoothly. He let me work without bothering me.

But every now and then, he surprised me.

One morning, he caught me singing softly while I wiped down the kitchen counters. I hadn't realised he was there until I heard his voice behind me.

"Didn't know I'd hired entertainment as well."

I turned around so quickly that I nearly dropped the dishcloth. He stood in the doorway, amusement dancing in his pale blue eyes.

"Sorry," I said, feeling embarrassed. "Bad habit. I forget people can hear me."

"I wouldn't call it bad," he replied, stepping closer. "You've got a nice voice, Jane."

The way he said my name felt casual, yet it carried a weight that landed deep inside me, making my stomach tighten.

I laughed it off, mumbling something about sticking to cleaning instead of performing. But when he walked by to grab his coffee mug, the light brush of his arm against mine sent a small shiver through my skin.

It was nothing. Completely harmless.

And yet, not.

***

Linine Langley

In the quiet hours of the afternoon, when the sun filters through the hallways and the house falls into silence, I often find myself thinking about him. Not about his appearance, though that would be simple, but about his calmness and steadiness. He moves through the world as if he has nothing to prove. After years of being with men who confused control with strength, Nate feels different. That difference is exactly what makes me uneasy.

***

One Thursday evening, he calls from the study while I finish the last of the dinner dishes.

"Jane, could you help me for a moment?"

He's at his desk, surrounded by files and notes, a furrow across his brow.

"Sorry to bother you," he says, "but I can't get this system update to work. You're better with technology than I am."

I lean over to look at the screen, careful to keep a polite distance. "You just need to restart it," I tell him. "You have too many programs running."

He laughs lightly. "Story of my life."

When I glance up, he's watching me closely.

"You have a calm way about you," he says after a moment. "It's rare."

I blink, caught off guard. "Calm? I don't think anyone's ever called me that before."

He smiles faintly. "Then they haven't been paying attention."

I don't know how to respond. The words are simple, but they go deeper than they should. I mumble something about returning to the kitchen and escape before I can betray the warmth rising in my cheeks.

That night, as I lie in bed, I think about his tone, the quiet certainty in it, the way it made me feel noticed. Too noticed, maybe.

***

Passionate Poison

Weeks pass, and the line between professionalism and familiarity begins to blur in small, almost invisible ways.

We share a laugh over burnt toast one morning. I receive a passing compliment about how efficiently I manage the place. We have a brief exchange about music, travel, and memories of places we've both seen.

These little things shouldn't mean much, yet together, they start to mean something.

There are moments when our hands brush as I pass him a cup, and neither of us pulls away right away. Sometimes, I catch him looking at me, not in appraisal, but in curiosity.

I tell myself it's just a human connection, two people working closely in the same space. Nothing more.

But late at night, when the house is quiet, I feel the echo of it, that undercurrent of possibility.

***

One Friday afternoon, Nate tells me he's hosting a small business conference the next day. "I'll need someone to help with arrangements overnight," he says, glancing at me across the table. "Would you be comfortable staying here for the evening?"

I nod a bit too quickly. "Of course."

"Good," he replies. "It'll just make things easier."

He says it plainly, but beneath his calm tone, I sense something else.

That night, I pack an overnight bag with practical items and drive up the hill, feeling a strange flutter of nerves in my chest.

The evening passes quietly. I help prepare the space, set out refreshments, and make sure the guest rooms are ready. Nate thanks me with a half-smile that lingers longer than usual.

By the time the last client leaves, the house quiets down comfortably.

Linine Langley

We sit at the long dining table, a single lamp casting soft light between us. He pours us each a glass of wine, saying it's "for a job well done."

The conversation begins light and easy. We talk about travel, work, and the view from the hill. Then, as the air settles and silence stretches, he leans back slightly and studies me.

"You know," he says, his voice low, "your eyes could look right into someone's soul."

The words linger in the quiet.

I want to laugh it off, to deflect, but something in his expression stops me. It's not a line or even really flirtation. It's a genuine observation.

"Maybe that's because I've seen a lot," I say softly.

His gaze holds mine for a moment longer. Then he nods, almost to himself. "Maybe."

The air feels different after that, not uncomfortable, just charged, as if the room is holding its breath.

I excuse myself soon after, citing tiredness. In truth, I need some space to breathe and think.

***

In my room, I sit on the edge of the bed and listen to the hum of the ceiling fan. My mind races.

It was just a compliment, I tell myself. Nothing more. But the way he said it and the way he looked at me stirred something I had tried so hard to quiet.

Desire, yes, but also fear.

I know what happens when I let someone in too far, too fast. I know how quickly warmth can turn to burn.

Yet, beneath all that caution, a spark flickers. It feels alive and daring.

Maybe this is what it's like to begin again. To stand at the edge of something that could heal me or break me open all over again.

Passionate Poison

I lie back and stare at the ceiling, my heart unsteady and my mind spinning.

The night stretches long and quiet.

Somewhere in the house, I hear Nate's footsteps retreat down the hall.

For a fleeting moment, I wonder if he's thinking about me too.

Then I close my eyes, uncertain, not of him, but of myself.

Maybe the real question isn't whether he'll cross that line.

Maybe it's whether I will.

Chapter Two: What Next

The morning after the conference dawns heavy and still.

The air is distinct, denser perhaps, laden with something that hovers between memory and potential. I navigate the kitchen softly, hoping to anchor myself in the cadence of tiny chores. Kettle on. Mugs from the cabinet. Toast in the tray. Prosaic things.

But nothing is normal.

Everything sounds crisper: the rasp of the blade against the plate, the hum of the refrigerator, the creaking echo of footsteps from the floor above. I know those footsteps. I see the hesitation before the landing that they take, the slowing near the last step.

Nate appears in the doorway a moment afterwards, bare feet, shirt sleeves rolled, hair a bit mussed. It shouldn't all equate to anything; it's early, it's casual, it's warm. But it causes my heart to skip a beat.

"Morning," he states, his voice still rough from slumber.

"Good morning." I try a small smile. "Coffee?"

"Please," he replies.

He's by the counter while I pour. The silence stretches, not awkward, exactly, but packed full of all that's left unspoken. I hand him the mug, and our hands brush for a second, the fleeting zip that goes between us nearly electric.

He doesn't step aside.

"Did you sleep all right?"

He asks me across the rim of his cup.

I nod. "Late, later than I should have."

His lips are slightly curved, as if he understands precisely. "Good."

Passionate Poison

We stand for a moment longer, neither of us quite sure where to go. The light from the window illuminates the tiles of the kitchen in a patch of gold, the suspended thoughts suspended mid-air.

One can step back, laugh, and change the direction of the moment. But something in his gaze freezes me.

I couldn't breathe easily.

***

The day fractures into moments, extended moments that are electric, near-filmic. The brush of his shoulder when he moves past me in the hall. The warm inflection in his voice when he says thank you for some mundane thing. The glance between our eyes across a room, and we both don't look away soon enough.

By afternoon, I am agitated. I settle in the garden, feigning to work a patch of rosemary that doesn't need it. The air is warm and pungent. I am incapable of settling.

What am I doing?

I've structured my world around rules ever since the divorce: *be careful, remain vigilant, don't blur boundaries.* And yet here I am, pounding heart like a teenager's, consciousness of every second that he's around.

The sound of gravel behind me makes me jump out of my trance. I look around. Nate is standing there, hands shoved in his pockets, a small smile tugging his lips.

"Having a bit of a break, are we?" he asks.

"Something like that," I answer playfully.

He grins and takes a step forward, the light from the afternoon catching in his hair. "You've accomplished a lot here," he says. "The building feels, what's the word, homely. I am not sure if that's a word"

I shrug, or I attempt to. "Perhaps it required a woman's touch."

"Maybe," he says softly. "Or, maybe it's just you."

I look him in his eyes then, and the world comes to a halt. No wind. No sound. The gentle thrum of air and heartbeats.

Something shifts, small but irreversible.

He doesn't touch me, not yet. But his nearness, the heat coming off the two of us, is its own kind of touch.

I can walk away. I have to.

But I don't.

***

That evening, the sky turns bruised and heavy with rain. Thunder rolls across the hills as the first drops hit the windows.

Inside, the house is cocooned, soft and golden lamplight, a long stretch of shadows. Nate's sitting in the study when I move by to close the curtains. He glances up when I enter the room, dark-eyed and thoughtful.

"The power could fail; outages are commonplace during thunderstorms," I say. "I'll check the generator."

"Leave it," he says. "It'll hold."

He rises then, stepping to the window next to me. For a moment, both of us observe the rain running down the glass, two silent figures between light and darkness.

All of a sudden, he looks at me.

"Jane."

It's not the word itself that undoes me, it's the way he says it. Low, certain, almost like a question and a statement at once.

I look at him, my heart pounding.

Neither of us breathes for a second. Then he gets closer, slowly, deliberately, until I can feel the warmth of his breath, the faint scent of coffee and rain on his flesh, his body.

"It feels." I start, but the words jam.

Passionate Poison

"Real," he concludes softly.

And I nod until I manage to restrain myself.

What follows isn't scripted or hurried or even terribly comprehensible. It's that type of moment that occurs outside of logic, two human beings passing a boundary that neither of them originally intended to cross.

His hand finds mine, tentative at first, then sure. The contact is simple, almost chaste, but it holds a weight that steals the air from the room. I can feel the tremor in my own breath, the answering steadiness in his.

There are no words. Everything that matters has already been said, in the look we share, the wordless giving of space, the unspoken *yes*.

We sit for so long like that, close enough together that we feel the shape of the moment, the current between us. The rain pounds more insistently against the panes, and the world outside fades away.

***

Sometime later, minutes, perhaps hours, I don't know, I sit in the quiet of my own room, the after-effects ringing in.

Everything feels unreal. The air is thick with the shadow of what's occurred, a touch, an exchange, a boundary crossed not with carelessness but with awareness.

It wasn't lust. It was something more, something quieter, the coming together of two people who'd each grown tired of acting like they didn't *feel*.

And yet, beneath the soft hum of heat, fear begins to roil. *What's next?*

I look in the mirror. My face is the same, and somehow, different. There's flush in my cheeks, softness in my eyes. I look alive.

But with it, the familiar pull of doubt. I've been here before, let my heart open, disregarded the warnings, assured myself this time things were somehow different.

And there I am once more, at the edge of something which I am only in part comprehending.

Linine Langley

The idea of morning and beholding him turns my stomach, hope and fear twisted together. *What if it's different? What if it's too late?*

Outside, the storm shifts and begins to subside. I sit at the window, the clouds parting in soft silver fragments.

I think of his voice, calm and steady, the way it gentled as he spoke *my* name.

It wasn't lust, no, not even that. It was recognition. Recognition of who I am, of what I need, of what propels me forward. Something that made me feel noticed, really noticed, for the first time in years.

And perhaps that's why I fear the most.

Because even after all my rebuilding with caution, after all the resilience I've found in loneliness, I simply cannot get rid of the apprehension that I've left open a door which shall never be closed.

The house is still. I listen to the rhythmic dripping from the rainfall off the eaves, the distant thudding from the closing door somewhere down the hall.

I remind myself to sleep, to let it rest till morning. But sleeping shall be hard, no, not when each thought, each beat of the heart guides me towards him.

Nate.

The person whose self-assurance frightens me.

The man whose calm entices.

The man who, with no promise at all, has already changed the shape of my world.

The first thing that comes into my consciousness when I wake up is the quiet. Stillness, almost ringing silence.

No storm, no roaring, no tapping at the windows with the rain, only that soft early-morning quiet which is calm and unsettling at once. For an instant, I am lying supine with my eyes shut and trying to relearn the art of breath once more.

Passionate Poison

It all comes back in flashes: the passion in his touch, the way he'd looked at me as if he were beholding through every wall I ever built, the silence that spoke more than words ever could.

And now, in the light of dawn, the burden of it all is real.

What have I done?

The thought isn't regret, really, but one of incredulity. Last night is impossibly close and far off at once, like a dream receding to darkness. Slowly, I get up, run fingers through my hair, and try to still the thudding in my pulse.

Then there's a gentle knock at the door.

"Jane? Breakfast is served."

Nate's voice, level, even, impassive.

I swallow again. "Thanks. I'll be down soon."

He does not reply. Nothing but the distant echo of his footsteps in the corridor.

***

The kitchen smells of coffee and toast. He's in the kitchen when we enter, ready for work, crisp workshirt, cufflinks, the whole nine yards. He's the epitome of calm. If I didn't know better, I'd take an oath that completely nothing had changed.

"Morning," I get out.

"Morning," he says, glancing up at him with a friendly smile and then back at his tablet. "Sleep okay?"

"Yes. You?"

"Alright."

Small talk, completely innocent, but every word carries its weight, precariously poised in the balance of something unsaid. The mood is varied. Not cold, but circumspect.

I spread my butter on my toast intentionally, too careful in making sure it's evenly coated. He reads his mail, sipping at a cup of coffee in the same manner he does each morning. Only it's not *like* every other morning, and we are well aware of the fact.

When he finally does look up, he stares at me for a moment, then turns his head.

"I'll be busy all day," he tells me. "A sequence of meetings in the city. You'll have the house all day yourself."

I nod, trying to be casual. "No problem."

That's it. He stands up, finishes his coffee, grabs his keys, and he's off with a simple "See you later."

The door closes behind him. The quiet that comes is massive.

***

The hours elapse. I clean, I cook, I wash, all the usual things, but my head can't calm down. Everything feels like waiting. Everything that hits the door makes me sit up in my chair, hoping to hear him talk again.

I remind myself not to be stupid. It was just one night, a flash of connection in an unpredictable world. But even while I attempt to rationalise it away, a part of me can't help but wonder what's going through his head.

Does he regret it?

Does he ever entertain the thought the same way that I do?

By late afternoon, I shed the pretense of being productive and set off on a lengthy walk down the hill. The aroma is damp earth and gum leaves, the pavement still damp from the rainfall the night before. It's quiet enough so that I can hear my own thoughts, which, it happens, aren't always a blessing.

***

When I return, he's home. His car is in the drive, the front light on.

Passionate Poison

I take a breath before walking inside.

He's in the lounge, phone in hand, suit jacket draped over a chair. When he looks up, his expression is warm, friendly, and even, but there's still that measured distance in his tone.

"Hey," he says. "You disappeared for a bit."

"Just went for a walk."

"Good idea." He gestures toward the kitchen. "I ordered takeaway if you're hungry."

We share a meal, talk lightly, work, weather, and the terrible traffic on the M1. Nothing regarding last night. Nothing personal. It's nearly too mundane.

I chuckle when he grumbles about cricket, his side lost by miles.

"Serves you right," I mock. "You should've supported the right team."

"Oh, so you're an expert now?"

"Better than you, obviously."

The banter feels easy, natural, like a reset button has been pressed. But beneath the laughter, something remains. A flicker. A hum. The awareness that we're both *pretending* a little.

***

Life falls back into routine over the next few weeks.

He works long hours; I look after the house, the garden, the quiet routine of life. Sometimes we eat together or watch a bit of Netflix. It's cosy, even pleasant, though sometimes I catch him staring at me with that same quiet intensity, as if he's remembering too.

Then he'll grin, change the subject, and it passes.

I begin to spend more time with friends, familiar faces I haven't seen in years. We have beers, swap tales, and laugh at the mistakes of the past. I remain carefree, even when they press me about my new job.

Linine Langley

"So, what's the boss man like?" one of them asks one evening at the pub.

I hesitate a beat too long. "He's... fine. Keeps to himself. Bit of an enigma, really."

They smile knowingly, friends do. "Ooh, that sounds interesting."

I brush it off, but within me, something curls up tight. It's safer not to have to tell someone what I don't even understand myself.

***

Weeks pass. Nate and I stop feeling so awkward with each other, and instead, a silence between us develops, a silence that is almost perilously comforting.

We begin to speak more, about all and nothing. Books, journeys, family, the odd ways human beings come apart and then find themselves. He listens, really listens, and I realise how unusual this is.

Sometimes, late in the evening, we'll sit on the veranda with a glass of wine, watching the lights of the city shimmer in the distance. The conversation flows easily, touched by a warmth that feels both safe and charged.

One night, after a stretch of silence, he says softly, "You seem different lately. Happier."

I glance at him, caught off guard. "Do I?"

"Yeah," he says, smiling faintly. "It suits you."

I look away, not trusting my voice. "Maybe I'm just getting used to things."

"Maybe," he replies, but there's something thoughtful in his tone. Something that makes my chest tighten.

***

There's a rhythm now, laughter over morning coffee, teasing comments about who left the dishes out, the occasional shared glance that lingers just a moment too long.

Passionate Poison

We take drives on the weekends, no place to go, just twisty roads and partially completed sentences. One time, when the car stalled, we sat on the bonnet munching on chips, giggling like morons while we waited for the tow. It was normal, and yet I couldn't recall the last time I felt so… alive.

He speaks of his work, his travels, his crabby dog who lives with his ex. I listen, observing how his eyes relax when he speaks of things that are important to him.

And yet, despite all the laughter and comfort, there's still a line neither of us crosses again.

Sometimes I question whether we're both too cautious, two souls circling around what we both desire but too afraid to grab it.

Other days, I think perhaps that's what it's supposed to be: soft connection, consistent companionship, the type of intimacy that doesn't require definition.

***

It's late, and I'm turning off the lights and going to bed, when he speaks up from the study.

"Jane?"

"Yeah?"

He looks up from his desk, that small, knowing smile in place. "Thanks for… everything. You've made this place feel like home again."

For a moment, the words hang there, soft and sincere.

I smile back, my heart tightening in that familiar, helpless way. "You're welcome, Nate."

And as I walk to my own room, I notice something's changed again, quietly, subtly. Not back to the intensity of that one night, but in a direction deeper.

Not passion, not yet.

But *understanding*.

Linine Langley

A sort of trust that doesn't have to be said.

***

I used to believe that I was skilled at holding back. At sensing when to draw the line, when to recede before things got too messy. But with Nate, the line's gotten fuzzy, soft-edged and moving, like a drawing in sand that the tide washes away.

It's not an attraction anymore. It's something more elusive, a low hum that settles in my chest when I hear his voice, the *heat* that rises when he smiles at me.

And now, that heat is beginning to feel like it could hurt me.

We've fallen into a comfortable rhythm: morning coffee, quick chats before he leaves for meetings, the odd shared meal in the evenings. It's easy, familiar, but threaded with something unspoken.

One night, we're sitting on the veranda after dinner. The cicadas are singing their hearts out, the air heavy with summer humidity. He's relaxed, drink in hand, a few shirt buttons undone.

"I'm not exactly the marrying kind," he states abruptly, as though he's reading my mind. "Never have been."

The words are a surprise. "Oh?"

He shrugs. "Just never seemed worth it, I guess. Relationships become complicated. People shift."

I let out a tiny laugh that's more cracked than I mean. "You don't say."

He looks at me, his smile faltering. "You do know what I'm saying. It's not that I don't care about people. I just… I've learned not to promise things I don't do." There's truth in his words, but a sort of finality, a door quietly shutting. I nod, acting as if I know everything, though something within me drops.

Later that evening, as I'm in bed, his words whirl around my mind like moths to a fire.

Passionate Poison

I remind myself it doesn't matter. That I don't want anything *serious*, that's what we share, this odd, silent chemistry, is sufficient.

But in my heart, I know that's not the case.

***

A few days pass, and life deals me a curveball.

My phone rings in the middle of the afternoon. It's Kate, a friend of mine whom I haven't laid eyes on for months. Her voice shakes when she speaks.

"Jane, I don't want to ask, but… will you come over? It's just been one of those days. I don't want to be alone."

I don't hesitate. "Of course. I'll be right over."

When I say to Nate that I'll be away overnight, he doesn't respond much. Just a soft "Right," followed by a silence long enough to feel like an unfinished question hanging in the air.

"She's going through a tough spot," I explain, picking up my bag. "I'll call tomorrow."

He nods, his face blank but his voice just a little off. "Do what you have to do."

I pause. "You, okay?"

"Yeah, sure." He gives a smile that falls just short of his eyes. "Drive safely."

But as I drive down the driveway, I can sense the change between us, small, but there.

***

Kate's apartment is a disaster, with wine glasses on the counter, half-open boxes, and a mess of bad choices she's attempting to laugh her way out of. I spend the night listening, comforting, and making her tea when she's out of tears.

But even as she speaks, my mind continues to wander back to Nate. To the glance he shot me as I departed, the manner in which he spoke the words "Drive safe" as if swallowing the remainder of the sentence.

When I eventually burrow into Kate's guest bed, the quiet is too vociferous.

***

By the time I come back the following afternoon, there is a change in the air at home. Nate's vehicle is in the driveway, but the front door is closed. I enter, my gut cramping with something akin to guilt.

He's in his office, working away, not glancing up when I arrive.

"Hey," I whisper.

"Hey."

His voice is polite, faraway. The sort that informs me he's annoyed, even if he won't say so.

"How was your friend?"

"She's okay. Just needed to talk."

He grunts and continues typing. "Good."

I wait for more, but the silence hangs between us like a thin, non-frangible thread.

Eventually, I sigh. "You're annoyed."

He puts down his fingers and leans back, looking at me. "No. I'm just… surprised you didn't tell me you'd be out all night."

"I didn't know I would be. It wasn't intentional."

He nods once more, but the jaw muscle clenches. "Right."

And suddenly, I feel tiny, like I've done something bad when I haven't.

I want to say to him, I missed you. I thought of you all the time I was away. But the words catch in my throat.

Instead, I say, "I'll get dinner started," and exit the room.

Passionate Poison

***

The tension hangs around for days, tense, bubbling, unresolved.

He's courteous but reserved. I echo his tone, reminding myself that it's okay, that I owe him nothing. But the reality is, the silence between us is denser than words.

Soon, one night, I discover a note on the kitchen counter in his handwriting:

Gone into the city. Late finish. Don't wait up.

Ordinary. Detached.

But it lands harder than I anticipate.

I clean the house, cook for one, and pour a glass of wine I hardly sip. The evening drags out, the clock ticking louder than it needs to.

It's almost midnight when my phone vibrates.

A text. From him.

Couldn't sleep. Are you awake too?

My heart flails.

Yeah. You're okay?

There's silence, then:

Missed talking to you.

I look at the screen, not knowing what to respond. Then I type:

You could've just said that to my face.

Silence again.

Did not think I was entitled to.

Something in me relaxes. I don't respond for a long while, just sit in the silence, looking at the letters shining on the screen.

When I do, finally, it is brief:

You don't need my permission to talk to me, Nate.

Linine Langley

***

The morning after, everything is different once more, not really fixed, but better.

He smiles at me weakly over breakfast, and the tension finally eases for the first time in days.

We talk about nothing, weekend plans, weather, groceries, but the expression in his eyes says far more than words ever could.

Later, as he is leaving the door, he hesitates.

"Jane?"

"Yeah?"

"Thanks… for understanding."

I nod, holding his eyes. "Always."

He pauses for an extra moment, and then smiles that small, knowing smile, the one that makes me lose track of how to breathe correctly.

And then he's vanished.

***

That evening, I'm lying awake once again, gaping up at the ceiling.

I ponder the last few weeks, the closeness, the confusion, the small cracks that keep emerging and somehow persisting.

It's dirty. Unstable. Unknowable.

And yet, I feel like I'm in precisely the right place.

Perhaps it isn't about discovering something flawless. Perhaps it's discovering how to exist within the messiness, the times of quiet, the laughter, the glances that linger too long.

As I doze off to sleep, my phone vibrates once again.

One line only.

Still up?

A grin creeps onto my mouth.

Passionate Poison

I reply, stupid but real: *Was just thinking of you.*

Chapter Three: The Trip

Life had settled into a rhythm I hadn't had in years. Not a predictable one, because nothing with Nate was ever entirely predictable, but a steady kind of emotional pulse. Work around the house kept me busy in that satisfying way where, by the time evening came, I could look around and actually feel like I'd achieved something. Evenings were quieter now; sometimes we'd talk, sometimes we wouldn't. When we did, it was easy, teasing, subtle, layered. When we didn't, it still didn't feel uncomfortable. It was simply… an unspoken understanding.

I'd been thinking about taking some leave for a while. Not because I was burnt out exactly, but because I wanted to breathe differently for a bit, somewhere far from my own thoughts bouncing around these walls. Tasmania had always been on my radar; something about crisp mornings, quiet beaches, and empty stretches of coastline appealed to me. I imagined walking alone with my coffee, salt air in my lungs, trying to sort through all the feelings I wasn't really naming yet.

So one morning, while Nate sat at the kitchen bench looking over some paperwork, I took a breath and said, "I'm thinking about taking some leave soon. A week, maybe. Tasmania."

I expected a quick nod, maybe a casual "Sounds good, enjoy it." What I didn't expect was the pause. The paper froze mid-page-turn. He didn't look at me straight away, just stared at his document for a second too long.

"Tasmania," he repeated eventually. Not a question. More like an evaluation.

I tried to keep it light. "Yeah. Somewhere quiet. Bit of a reset."

Another pause. Then a short, clipped: "Right."

Just that. No enthusiasm. No casual encouragement. No neutral acceptance. Just… right. As if I'd told him I'd be gone indefinitely, leaving him to figure things out alone.

Passionate Poison

He shifted topics almost immediately, asking if I'd emailed the cleaner about supplies. It was like I hadn't said anything of value.

I spent the rest of the day going back and forth in my head. Was he annoyed? Didn't care? Pretending not to care? Or just busy? Had I misread everything between us again? I tried to shrug it off, but every time I caught sight of him passing through a hallway or speaking to me in a tone too normal, it felt strained in a way I couldn't quite place.

By late afternoon, he was quieter than usual. Not cold, just distant, the kind of distance you notice more because you're used to him being aware of you. That awareness seemed switched off, or hidden behind some internal wall.

In my room that night, scrolling through flights and cute Airbnbs near the Tasmanian coast, I couldn't shake the unsettled feeling.

Was I overthinking this? Probably. Definitely. Maybe.

The next morning, Nate barely looked at me over breakfast but mentioned, in that annoyingly composed voice, "Let me know the dates when you've booked."

I nodded, waiting for more. There wasn't any.

Later that afternoon, while ironing freshly washed sheets, I overheard him on the phone in his office. His tone was different, low, firm, talking logistics. A name I didn't know, something about availability, then, "Yes, that'll work. She'll be there on Monday."

She. I didn't think anything of it at first.

An hour later, he appeared in the doorway where I was cleaning one of the upstairs bathrooms.

"I've arranged accommodation for you," he said casually, as though he hadn't just steamrolled my independence like it was nothing.

I blinked. "Sorry... what?"

"For Tasmania. You'll stay with an associate of mine. It's private, quiet. Better than some random holiday rental."

I stared at him, cloth still in hand. "You organised my accommodation without asking?"

He held my gaze without flinching. "Yes."

I opened my mouth, closed it again. "You just decided where I'd stay?"

"Decided where you'd be safest," he corrected calmly, as if that made it entirely different.

There was a stretch of silence between us. My chest was tight with a weird cocktail of feelings, annoyance, frustration, confusion... and, stupidly, something warm I didn't want to acknowledge.

"I can handle booking my own trip, Nate."

"I know," he said. "But I prefer knowing where you are."

I looked at him for a long moment, trying to decipher whether he meant that in a practical, employer-like way or something more protective. I couldn't decide if it was controlling or caring. Maybe it was both. That made it more complicated.

I didn't say thank you. I also didn't undo what he'd done.

Two days later, I left.

The flight was early, and the house felt too big and echoey when I walked through it with my suitcase. Nate was already awake, standing in the kitchen with coffee like he always did. He didn't offer to drive me. I didn't expect him to.

"Have a safe trip," he said, voice neutral.

"Thanks," I said quietly.

There was a pause long enough for something more to happen, a longer look, a touch, a sign, but neither of us crossed that line.

The car pulled up outside, and I left without looking back.

When the plane was taking off, I pressed my forehead against the window and watched Brisbane shrink beneath the clouds, that twist in

Passionate Poison

my stomach refusing to ease. I should've been excited, Tasmania was beautiful even in my imagination. Freedom, salt air, fresh perspective.

But instead, I kept replaying his voice in my head: *I prefer knowing where you are.*

Was that possessive? Protective? A sign he cared? Or just Nate needing control in every situation, even when it came to my leave?

When I landed, Tasmania was everything I expected: cold, crisp, beautifully detached from everything else. The coastline looked like it had been carved for reflection. The silence felt full of possibility.

But even standing there with my bags and the scent of sea air curling around me, I couldn't stop thinking about Nate, his silence, his control, his distance, and that one line that sat under my ribs like something warm I didn't want and couldn't ignore.

***

The motel Nate had arranged was nicer than I'd expected, not flashy, but clean, modern, and perched on a quiet stretch of coastline where the ocean sounded close enough to touch. The view alone felt like a deep exhale. I unpacked slowly, trying to settle into the silence, telling myself I needed this time to think without distractions, to get my head straight.

But the silence made space for thoughts I didn't want to unpack yet.

I went for a walk along the beach that afternoon. The sand was cold and fine beneath my sneakers, the wind sharp enough to sting my cheeks. I wrapped my jacket tighter around me and tried to let the rhythm of the waves clear my mind. It helped, but only slightly. Nate was still there in the back of my mind, like a song I couldn't switch off.

By the time I got back to the room, my mood had settled into something softer but still unsettled. I opened the door, half-thinking about a hot shower and maybe ordering dinner, when I stopped.

There was something on the bed.

Linine Langley

A bouquet, deep, warm tones, nothing overly romantic but intentionally chosen, not the sort you grab on a whim. Next to it sat a small, square box wrapped neatly in dark paper with a simple string bow.

My first thought was that housekeeping had mixed up rooms. My second thought was worse, that someone had been in here without permission for some creepy reason. My heartbeat picked up. I looked around quickly; everything else seemed untouched, but my sense of calm had flickered out.

I moved slowly towards the bed, hesitating before picking up the card resting on top of the flowers.

> *No need to overthink this. Just enjoy your week.*
>
> *N.*

I froze.

N.

My mind rushed through a thousand reactions: confusion, annoyance, warmth, shock, disbelief. I let out a breath I hadn't realised I was holding and just stood there, staring at the card like it might explain itself.

There was a knock at the door.

I didn't move straight away. Something inside me already knew who it was, before my body caught up to that truth.

I opened the door.

Nate stood there, casual as ever. Jeans, jacket, hands in pockets like this was no big deal. His hair looked windswept, his usual calm expression edged with something more cautious, as if he was prepared for me to slam the door in his face.

"What are you doing here?" I asked, my voice too soft to match the pounding in my chest.

He didn't step forward, just observed me. "I flew down this morning."

Passionate Poison

"I gathered that," I said, a bit breathlessly. "But… why?"

He held my gaze, steady as always. "Because you were here."

I blinked, my throat tightening. "That's not a reason."

"It is to me."

I swallowed hard. There were so many words hovering between us that I didn't know which one to catch first. I glanced over my shoulder at the flowers. "You could've just sent the flowers."

"I did." He paused. "And then I got on a plane."

I didn't know whether to be angry, relieved, overwhelmed, or all of them at once. He took a quiet breath, as though giving me space to process.

Eventually, I stepped back. He walked in.

The room suddenly felt smaller. He didn't move far, just stood in the middle of the space, looking at me as though checking if he'd gone too far.

"You could've told me you were coming," I said quietly.

"I wasn't sure you'd want me to," he replied, voice low. "But I wasn't going to sit at home thinking about whether you were okay. Or who you were with. Or whether you'd decided you were better off without all… this."

He didn't gesture, but I felt what *this* meant. The space between us. The unfinished conversations. The uncertainty. The quiet gravity that had been pulling me toward him even when I tried to walk away.

"I wasn't running from you," I said softly.

He nodded. "I know. But I didn't want you to feel like you had to be alone to think clearly. I'd rather you… thought clearly with me there."

There was no arrogance in his tone, just honesty. Vulnerable, quiet honesty. It disarmed me more than anything else could have.

I sat on the edge of the bed. "So what are we doing, Nate?" I asked, my voice barely above a whisper.

He looked at me, expression unreadable but open. Then he sat beside me, not too close, but close enough that I could feel his warmth.

"That depends," he said. "On whether you're ready to hear that I care about you more than I planned to."

My chest tightened. He continued, voice steady.

"I don't do this," he said quietly. "I don't chase people. I don't show up in other states because I can't stop thinking about whether someone's sleeping properly or if they're overthinking everything alone at night."

My eyes stung unexpectedly.

"I'm not saying I have it all figured out," he added. "But I know I don't want to pretend this doesn't matter."

Something inside me, something tightly coiled, loosened, just a fraction.

"I'm scared," I admitted, my voice shaking slightly.

"I know," he said. "So am I."

We sat in silence, letting the truth settle between us. It wasn't dramatic or rushed, just real.

After a while, I asked, "So where does that leave us?"

He looked at me gently. "Here," he said. "Figuring it out. Honestly."

The rest of the evening passed quietly, not in avoidance, but in comfort. We talked properly, about trust, expectations, fears we rarely said out loud. There were no big declarations, just steady honesty.

When he finally reached for my hand, it wasn't possession. It was reassurance.

We chose to stay together that night, not in a blaze of physical intensity, but wrapped in emotional stillness that felt strangely safe. There was warmth, quiet closeness, and the soft understanding that something between us had shifted, not towards chaos this time, but towards clarity.

Passionate Poison

As I drifted to sleep with the sound of distant waves somewhere beyond the window and Nate breathing quietly beside me, I realised I wasn't scared in the same way anymore.

We hadn't solved everything.

But we'd stopped pretending we didn't care.

And that changed everything.

***

The last morning in Tasmania wasn't supposed to be the last. We'd planned another day of wandering along the coast, maybe grabbing breakfast at that little café Nate had unexpectedly liked, pretending for a bit longer that we were just two people on holiday without real lives pressing in.

But life didn't ask for permission.

Nate was on his phone early, standing near the window with that tight jaw he gets when he's dealing with work. His voice was low, controlled, but the tone was unmistakably sharp. He ended the call and didn't speak for a minute, just stared out at the grey-blue water like he was trying to steady something inside himself.

"What's happened?" I asked quietly.

He turned to me, expression unreadable but firm. "We need to head back."

I blinked. "Today?"

"Yes."

There wasn't anger in his voice, just decision. Final. Immovable. The kind of tone that came from someone used to being in control and expecting others to fall into step.

I hesitated. "Do you… want me to fly back separately? I can stay and finish my leave."

His gaze sharpened instantly. "No," he said, too quickly. Then, softer, "Come back with me."

It wasn't a request. Not entirely. There was a protective edge to it, but also something bordering on possessive. I didn't fight it, though a part of me wondered why. Maybe because deep down, I already knew I would follow, no matter how much I pretended independence came first.

The flight back felt different to when I'd arrived. I sat by the window, watching the landscape blur into clouds, and felt the silent shift between us. Nate rested his hand on mine for most of the journey, warm, steady, but he didn't say much. His mind was already elsewhere, back in Brisbane, back in responsibility. I didn't push. But I felt the distance, subtle but present.

When we landed, everything moved quickly. Taxi. House on the hill. Bags dropped by the door. Nate took another phone call almost immediately, walking into his office without a backward glance.

I stood in the foyer alone, suddenly unsure of where I was supposed to go now.

Had something changed, or had we slipped back into the old patterns, with new feelings tucked quietly in our pockets like contraband?

Over the next couple of days, he was busy. Meetings. Calls. Barely home for dinner. When we did cross paths, he was warm, a quiet hand on my back, a soft "you okay?". But there was something else too, an intensity that made me feel watched, not in a creepy way, but in a "you're mine and I'm not sure how to say that" kind of way.

I wasn't sure how I felt about it.

I took a day off to catch up with Monique. We met at our favourite café, a casual spot with noisy mismatched chairs and the best flat whites in Brisbane. She raised an eyebrow the moment she saw me.

"You look different," she said, studying me. "Lighter. Or maybe more tangled. Can't tell yet."

I laughed. "Probably the second one."

Passionate Poison

We chatted about everything except him for a while, her new job, her ridiculous neighbour, and life. But eventually, she leaned forward, eyes narrowing.

"So, are we going to get to the part where you tell me about him?"

I hesitated. "It's complicated."

"Jane," she said firmly. "It's always complicated with you. That's why I'm asking."

I sighed. "I think... I think I care about him more than I meant to."

"Do you think he feels the same?"

I looked down at my hands. "Yes. But I don't know what to do with that."

"Why?"

"Because caring about someone means they can hurt you," I said quietly. "And I don't know if I'm ready for that again."

She was silent for a moment. Then she said, "You can't half-feel someone and hope that protects you."

Her words stayed with me long after I left.

The shift came unexpectedly one evening. Nate came home early, which was rare. I was in the kitchen making tea when he walked in. He didn't say hello straight away, just leaned against the counter, studying me.

"What were you doing today?" he asked lightly.

"Catching up with Monique," I said. "We went to the café on Oxford Street."

"With her boyfriend or just you?"

"Just me," I said, a bit thrown.

He nodded slowly. "Anyone else there you felt like catching up with?"

It took me a second to realise what he was implying. My stomach tightened. "Are you asking if I was meeting someone else?"

He shrugged, but not carelessly. "I just want to know what's going on."

Something hot and sharp pricked inside me, not quite anger but close. "Do you think I'm lying to you?"

He paused. "No… I just—"

"You what?"

"I don't want to lose control of something before I've even figured out how to hold onto it," he said quietly.

The vulnerability in his voice caught me off guard, softening my defensiveness, but the unease stayed. I reached for my tea, my mind racing.

Was this care or control?

Fear or mistrust?

Love or something that might one day suffocate me?

That night, I lay in bed staring at the ceiling, listening to the quiet of the house. Nate was in his office again, working late. I felt something both beautiful and terrifying tightening around my heart.

I was already in too deep. I could feel it.

He was the kind of man who didn't give himself easily, but when he did, he held tight. And I wasn't sure whether that grip would make me feel safe or trapped.

The idea of walking away now hurts more than I expected.

The idea of staying, totally staying, scared me more than anything.

Love, I was starting to realise, wasn't soft or simple.

It was fire, warm when you were close enough, burning when you got too deep.

As sleep finally crept in, I found myself wondering not whether I loved him, but whether I was strong enough for what loving him might cost me.

Passionate Poison

Linine Langley

Chapter Four:
Passionate Poison: Is It More?

The room still smells like him, warm skin, a trace of cologne, the faint scent of candle wax that burned too long into the night. I lie there staring at the ceiling, listening to the rhythm of his breathing beside me. It should be comforting, but instead it feels heavy, almost rehearsed. The space between us feels thicker than it did a few hours ago.

I shift slightly, careful not to wake him, and study the outline of his back. Strong shoulders, hair slightly mussed, the slow rise and fall of his chest. It's a sight I've memorised a hundred times over, and yet this morning it feels different, distant. Like I'm watching a stranger occupy the same bed.

How can someone make you feel so alive one moment and so uncertain the next? Last night was a blur of heat and emotion, too much, maybe. And now, in the stillness of morning, I can't help but ask myself the question that's been circling my mind for weeks: *is this love, or am I just losing myself in the idea of it?*

I reach out, my hand hovering just above his skin, but I stop before I touch him. He turns over suddenly, pulling the sheet tighter around his waist, his back now to me. It's such a small movement, but it slices through the silence. The message feels clear, whatever was shared last night has been folded away neatly, tucked somewhere I can't reach.

A lump forms in my throat. I tell myself I'm imagining it, that he's just tired, that men have their moods. But deep down, I feel it, something's shifted.

When I finally drift back to sleep, the light is already creeping through the curtains. By the time I wake again, Nate's gone. The space beside me is cold. I hear the sound of running water and his voice, low and slightly off-key, humming some tune I don't recognise. He only sings when he's in a good mood. That should make me smile, but it doesn't. It makes me wary.

Passionate Poison

I slip on my dressing gown and pad softly towards the bathroom. The steam curls beneath the door, carrying his voice with it. I reach for the handle, intending to join him, to shake off whatever unease has lodged itself in my chest, but then I hear it.

His voice drops, quieter now, and it's not a tune he's singing anymore. It's words. A conversation.

"Yeah, darling... I'll see you soon."

My hand freezes on the doorknob. *Darling.*

I stand there, heart hammering, unsure if I've heard him right. But then he laughs, that soft, low laugh he saves for moments when he's charming someone.

He's talking to someone else. A woman.

I don't move. I can't. My stomach twists as snippets of the conversation drift through the door. Something about a business trip. Something about "making arrangements." And then silence.

My ears are ringing by the time the shower stops. I back away from the door, my pulse racing. Maybe it's innocent. Maybe "darling" is just a habit, a slip of the tongue. But even as I try to reason with myself, I can feel my thoughts splintering.

When he finally steps out, towel around his waist, he's as calm as ever, whistling, casual, untouched by the weight pressing on my chest.

"Morning, honey," he says, leaning down to kiss my cheek like nothing's wrong. "I'm heading out today, business trip up north. Might be gone a couple of days."

I nod, forcing a smile that feels brittle. "Oh. I didn't realise."

He shrugs. "It came up quick. Thought you might take a few days for yourself. Go to that resort you mentioned once, relax, switch off. I'll book it for you."

His tone is gentle, easy, but there's something practised in it. As if he's reading from a script. My chest tightens. Does he really think I'm that naïve?

"That's… thoughtful of you," I say slowly. My voice doesn't sound like mine.

He grins, that perfect, disarming grin, and brushes his fingers through my hair. "You deserve a break, Jane. We both do."

I hold his gaze, searching for something genuine behind those calm blue eyes, but all I see is composure. Controlled. Measured. Untouchable.

Inside, I'm burning.

I tell myself not to react, not to show my hand. If he is lying, if that phone call wasn't what I think it was, then I'll find out soon enough. For now, I'll play along.

"Alright," I say finally. "A few days away might be nice."

He smiles again, kisses the top of my head, and disappears into the other room to make his "arrangements." I stay where I am, gripping the edge of the dresser until my knuckles whiten.

The sound of his voice, that one word, *darling*, keeps echoing through my head.

By the time he returns, his suitcase is packed, his phone in hand. He looks every bit the successful, confident man, and I, somehow, feel smaller beside him.

"Enjoy your trip," he says. "I'll see you soon."

As the door closes behind him, I let out a shaky breath I didn't realise I'd been holding.

Something isn't right. I can feel it in my bones. But if Nate thinks he's the only one who can play games, he's wrong.

This time, I'll find out exactly who he's calling *darling*.

***

The drive to the resort feels longer than it should. Every kilometre is heavy with questions I can't quite silence. The sky's a dull silver, the kind that promises rain without ever delivering it, and the road winds

Passionate Poison

through bushland that feels almost too still. When I finally pull up at the gates, pale stone, manicured hedges, a view of the sea just beyond, my stomach twists.

It's beautiful here. Peaceful. Too peaceful.

The concierge greets me by name before I even open my mouth. "Welcome, Ms Collins. Mr Hawthorne's already made the arrangements."

Of course he has.

I smile politely, though my pulse skips. "He's here?"

The young woman nods, oblivious to the wave of confusion that crashes through me. I follow her through the grand entrance, past walls of pale timber and glass, until we reach the suite. When she leaves me with the key, I take a moment at the door, just breathing, trying to steady myself.

Inside, the suite is immaculate. Soft lighting, a bottle of champagne on ice, a bowl of strawberries, and flowers, white lilies, my favourite. There's music too, faint and slow, drifting from somewhere unseen. It's the kind of scene you'd find in a film, thoughtful, romantic, deliberate.

Only it doesn't feel like it's for me.

It feels staged.

I step further in, scanning the space, and then I see him.

Nate.

Standing by the balcony doors, one hand tucked into his pocket, the other holding a glass of wine as if he's been waiting for this exact moment. He turns, smiling, calm, charming, utterly in control.

My breath catches. "What are you doing here?"

He sets the glass down, his expression unreadable. "You didn't really think I'd let you come alone, did you?"

Linine Langley

There's a flash of irritation, sharp and immediate. "You told me this was a chance to relax. To have space."

He walks towards me slowly, that deliberate confidence that always makes it hard to think straight. "And I realised," he says quietly, "that space isn't what either of us needs right now."

I fold my arms, heat rising in my chest. "So you decided to surprise me? Like some sort of test?"

He stops just in front of me, close enough that I can smell the faint trace of his aftershave, cedarwood, smoke, something darker beneath it. "Don't ask questions tonight," he murmurs. "Just trust me."

Those words. They should comfort me, but instead they make my pulse quicken in all the wrong ways.

"Trust you?" I echo, my voice trembling despite the anger behind it. "You call another woman *darling* on the phone and then expect me to walk into this like nothing's happened?"

His expression shifts, not guilt, not quite, something more restrained. "Jane," he says evenly, "that call wasn't what you think. If you'd waited, you'd have known that."

"Then explain it," I demand.

He exhales softly, running a hand through his hair. "I will. Just… not tonight. Please."

There's a softness in his tone that shouldn't disarm me, but it does. I hate that it does. He reaches for my hand, and I let him, though every rational thought screams at me not to. His touch is warm, grounding.

"Come outside," he says gently.

We step out onto the balcony. The ocean spreads wide and silver under the setting sun, waves catching the last of the light. The breeze carries the scent of salt and jasmine from the garden below. It's beautiful, heartbreakingly so, and for a moment, I forget why I'm angry.

Nate's voice breaks the quiet. "I planned this to remind us what we are when we stop doubting everything."

Passionate Poison

I turn to him. "And what are we, exactly?"

He looks at me, eyes steady. "Something real. Something worth the mess."

I want to believe him. God, I do. But there's a knot in my chest that won't loosen. "You think trust is something you can orchestrate? Book a room, light a few candles, and make it all disappear?"

He shakes his head. "No. I think trust is choosing to stay when you have every reason to leave."

The words linger between us, heavy and intimate. For a long moment, neither of us speaks. Then he reaches out, brushing a stray strand of hair from my face. His touch is careful, deliberate.

I close my eyes. The air between us hums, not with desire exactly, but something rawer. Connection. Fear. Longing.

"I don't know if I can do this," I whisper. "I'm scared, Nate. Not of you, of me. Of how much you can undo me without even trying."

He exhales slowly, resting his forehead against mine. "Then let me try not to hurt you," he says quietly. "Let me prove it."

For a moment, I let myself breathe him in, his warmth, the steadiness of his heartbeat, the illusion that maybe everything's fine. Maybe this is what love really is: a series of small surrenders that feel like choices.

But deep down, I know better.

Even as I melt into the quiet of his arms, part of me is still watching, still wondering if what he gives is love, or performance. Whether this is connection… or control.

The line between them is so thin, it's almost invisible.

And I'm starting to realise I might already be on the wrong side of it.

***

The morning after feels quieter than it should. Sunlight filters through the curtains in soft lines, catching on the glass of half-empty champagne flutes from the night before. The suite still smells faintly of lilies and sea air, but the warmth from the night seems to have cooled into something I can't name.

Nate's already up, moving around the room, calm and efficient as if nothing has changed. He hums under his breath, that low tune he does when his mind's elsewhere. I watch him from the bed, sheets twisted around me, and for a moment it feels like I'm looking at a stranger I'm supposed to know.

He glances over his shoulder and smiles. "Morning, sleepyhead. You should stay in bed a bit longer. I'll grab us some coffee."

His tone is light, affectionate even, but there's a distance to it, like he's talking through glass. I nod, forcing a smile. "Sure."

When he leaves the room, I pull my knees up and rest my chin on them. Everything looks perfect, the view, the flowers, the memory of last night, yet something inside me feels slightly out of tune, like a song played half a beat too slow.

We drive back home in near silence. Nate talks about work, about meetings and plans and calls, but his words drift past me. My thoughts keep circling back to the moment he told me, *Don't ask questions. Just trust me.* The words felt tender then. Now they feel like a leash.

Back home, the house feels bigger than I remember. Colder too. Nate's warmth lingers, but only faintly, like perfume after someone's gone. He disappears into his office almost as soon as we arrive, phone pressed to his ear, voice sharp and focused.

That's when it hits me, how easily I fall back into orbit around him. I cook, clean, check the messages, wait for him to emerge. It's as if the resort never ended, only shifted scenes.

Later that afternoon, he finds me in the kitchen. "Hey," he says softly, "I'm heading off tomorrow. Brisbane for a few days. Big client pitch. I'll need you to manage things here."

There it is again, that steady calm, the control tucked neatly beneath the kindness.

I nod, though my stomach twists. "Right. Of course."

Passionate Poison

He smiles, kisses the top of my head, and walks away to pack. Just like that.

When the door finally closes behind him the next morning, the silence is deafening. I move around the house aimlessly, tidying things that don't need tidying, checking my phone for messages that don't come. It's only when the clock hits noon that I sit down and actually breathe.

The quiet feels heavy. Too heavy.

I call Monique.

She answers on the second ring. "Hey, stranger. You sound flat, what's happened?"

I hesitate. "Nothing really. Just… trying to figure out where I stand with Nate."

"Ah," she says knowingly. "The famous figuring-out stage."

I let out a weak laugh. "If that's what it is."

She pauses before speaking again, her voice softer now. "Jane, sometimes love feels like being drunk. It feels incredible, everything's bright and easy, until you realise you've lost control. *Then you're just trying not to fall over.*"

Her words land harder than I expect. I don't respond straight away, just listen to her breathing on the other end of the line.

After we hang up, I sit at the kitchen table, staring at my reflection in the dark surface of my tea. There's a dull ache behind my ribs, the kind that doesn't quite hurt but never really goes away either.

I think about Nate, about his gestures, his charm, the way he always seems two steps ahead. It's hard to know if it's because he cares or because he needs to be the one in control. Maybe both. Maybe neither.

By late evening, the house is quiet again. I light a candle in the living room, more for company than ambience, and pull out my journal. The pages are filled with messy handwriting and half-truths, but tonight I need to see the words in front of me.

Linine Langley

I write:

He makes me feel alive, but also small. He holds me like I'm his world, but sometimes I wonder if he even sees mine. Every gesture feels like a promise, but each one comes with a price, trust, silence, surrender.

I pause, tapping the pen against the page, the words forming before I can stop them.

Is this love, or am I just the reflection of what he wants to see?

The candle flickers, sending shadows across the walls, and I close the journal before I can write anything else. The question lingers in the air long after the flame goes out.

For a moment, I wish I could rewind, go back to before I met him, before everything became this tangle of longing and doubt. But I know it's too late for that.

Whatever this thing between us is, love, obsession, control, it's already taken root.

And as much as I want to believe I can still walk away, a part of me knows the truth:

What began as passion now feels like *poison*, beautiful, consuming, and impossible to leave…

Passionate Poison

Chapter Five: The Room

Work is hectic, the kind of day where everything piles up at once and you start counting down the minutes till you can breathe again. With Nate away on a business trip, I've been pushing myself harder than usual. Part of it is pride, I want him to see I can handle things. The other part is... well, if I'm honest, it's fear of disappointing him. He runs a tight ship, and I don't want to be the reason something slips through the cracks.

By six o'clock, I finally get a break to sort through the paperwork that's been building faster than I can file it. I sit at his desk, open a fresh stack of folders, and try to clear my head. That's when I see it, an invoice tucked almost deliberately deep in a folder marked for accounts.

A florist's receipt. Weekly orders. Three months straight.

And printed in bold: Dispatched from private residential address.

Not to the business.

Not to me.

But from someone's home.

My stomach tightens in that sharp, instinctive way you get when something isn't right but you can't name it yet. Flowers aren't unusual for him, Nate buys them for clients sometimes, the odd apology bouquet, even for me on occasion. But this? Regular. Hidden. And coming *from* a private address... not going *to* one.

Why hide it? Why tuck the invoice away like that?

I stare at the paper for a long moment, the office silent around me. The whole building feels empty this time of night. The air almost hums. I tell myself it's none of my business, he's my boss, not my partner. Even so, my heart twists, because we both know the lines between those roles have blurred beyond recognition.

Linine Langley

I place the invoice aside, but it burns the back of my mind. Every scenario I can think of is worse than the last, and the more I try to ignore it, the more it presses against me like a bruise.

I try burying myself in the rest of the folders, but my concentration is shot. Eventually, I gather one folder to take home, convincing myself it's harmless, just finishing the day's overflow. Nate will appreciate the effort, I tell myself.

I'm wrong.

That night, after I slip into my pyjamas and pour a glass of wine, my phone rings. I light up instantly, his name still does something to me I can't quite explain. The warmth lasts two seconds.

"What the bloody hell are you doing taking work home?" he snaps. No hello. No softness.

I freeze. "I just grabbed one folder, Nate. I thought."

"You thought wrong." His voice is sharp as glass. "My paperwork stays in the office. If you can't manage the load, I'll find someone who can. And don't go through anything else. Leave it."

Before I can respond, the line goes dead.

I call back. Once. Twice. Three times. Straight to voicemail.

I sit on the edge of my bed, stunned, like someone's pulled the floor out from under me. That wasn't stress. That wasn't irritation. That was something darker, something calculated, almost. It rattles me enough that I leave the folder untouched on the dining table and crawl into bed feeling like I've missed something important.

Sleep comes in fits, broken and restless.

In the morning, a knock at the door startles me. It's barely half-past seven. A courier stands there holding the biggest bouquet I've ever seen, an explosion of lilies and roses, wrapped in crisp white paper.

"For Jane," he says.

The card is handwritten, Nate's unmistakable scrawl:

Passionate Poison

To my beautiful princess,

Sorry for my outburst.

You know I think the world of you.

Your man,

Nate.

"Your man."

He signs it like that so easily.

The flowers smell sweet and overwhelming. I place them in a vase, but I don't feel comforted. If anything, the apology confuses me more. How can someone be so cruel one minute and so tender the next? It's emotional whiplash, sharp and dizzying.

I slip the card into my handbag, because I always keep the little things he gives me, even when I'm upset with him. Maybe especially then. Pathetic, really.

At work later, I open the folder I brought home. A loose sheet falls to the floor, another florist document. Same format. Same handwriting. Same private residential address.

Cold spreads across my chest.

This isn't coincidence. And it definitely isn't business.

I sit back in Nate's chair, staring at the paper. Something about it feels deliberate, like a puzzle piece that's meant to be found, but not understood.

Should I ask him?

Should I leave it?

Do I even want the truth?

Curiosity and dread knot together inside me. The more I tell myself to ignore it, the stronger the pull becomes. There's something going on here, something he doesn't want me to see.

And the terrifying part?

Linine Langley

I'm not sure if I'm more afraid he's lying to me… or of what happens if I confront him and he isn't.

Either way, the crack is there now, in my trust, in my certainty, in us.

And once a crack starts, it never really stops.

***

By the time I get back to work, my head is already buzzing. The invoices, his outburst, his apology, none of it fits together neatly, and the gaps between those pieces feel sharper than the pieces themselves. I keep telling myself I'm overthinking it, but the truth is I don't believe my own reassurance anymore.

I walk into Nate's office, the scent of his aftershave still lingering faintly in the air from days ago. It hits me the same way it always does, warm, familiar, unsettling in a way I can't explain. I place the slipped florist document on the desk, intending to tuck it back where I found it and pretend I never saw it.

But when I bend down to open the drawer, something catches my eye.

The bottom drawer, the one he keeps locked at all times, is sitting a fraction open. Barely enough to notice, unless you were looking directly at it. Unless you were already suspicious.

My heart thumps so loudly I'm sure someone outside the building could hear it.

I stare at the tiny gap, and every rational thought tells me to walk away. To respect the boundary. To not make things worse.

But the other part of me, the part that's been chewing on doubt for days, leans closer.

I hesitate, breathing slowly through the weight in my chest. Then I gently ease the drawer open a touch further, just enough to glance inside without disturbing anything.

A key.

Small, silver, gleaming faintly under the dim office lights.

Passionate Poison

And beside it, a compact, locked box. Matte black, heavy-looking, deliberate.

My skin prickles.

This isn't paperwork or business receipts.

This is private, deeply private.

I don't even get the chance to decide what to do next.

The office door clicks shut behind me.

My body jolts so hard I bang my knee on the desk. I turn around quickly, heart hammering.

Nate stands there, leaning against the closed door as he slips the key into the lock. The sound of it turning feels louder than it should be.

He doesn't look angry.

That almost makes it worse.

"Lose something, Jane?" His voice is low, calm, too calm.

I swallow. "I... dropped a paper. Just putting it away."

He studies me with that slow, deliberate gaze he uses when he's working someone out. When he wants them to squirm without ever raising his voice.

"Funny," he says quietly. "You look nervous."

I force myself to steady my breathing. "I'm not nervous. I'm just trying to finish the work I didn't get to last night."

He steps forward, the movement unhurried, measured. His presence fills the room, the way he carries himself, the certainty in his stride. Everything about him radiates control.

He places his hand on the edge of the desk, leaning in just enough that his face is inches from mine. His eyes search mine, slow and assessing.

"What were you looking for, Jane?"

My throat tightens. "Nothing."

"Mmm." He tilts his head slightly. "You're not very good at lying."

He reaches past me and gently slides the drawer shut with one finger. Not slamming it. Not snapping. Just… closing it. Softly.

The softest things can feel the most threatening.

I take a slow breath. "Nate, I wasn't going through your things. I just…"

He cuts me off, his voice still unsettlingly quiet.

"I saw you."

My heart drops.

"Saw me what?" I manage.

"Going through my desk yesterday. And today."

He taps the corner of the ceiling lightly with his chin. "Cameras. Office security. You know how much I value order."

A shiver runs down my spine. Not from fear alone, something deeper, more complicated. The feeling of being exposed. Watched. Known too closely.

"I wasn't doing anything wrong," I whisper.

He steps even closer. "Then why do you look guilty?"

My pulse thrums so hard it's almost painful.

He runs a hand slowly along the desk, his fingers brushing mine, the touch feather-light but charged. Not sexual, not aggressive, just enough pressure to remind me how easily he can unbalance me.

"You don't trust me, do you?" he asks softly. "Is that what this is?"

The question cuts straight through me, sharp and clean. I don't answer. I can't. Because I'm not sure of the answer myself.

He watches my silence with a small, knowing smile.

"That's alright," he murmurs. "If you're unsure… I'll show you."

I blink. "Show me what?"

Passionate Poison

Instead of replying, he steps back and moves toward the tall bookshelf against the wall. I've walked past it a hundred times. There's nothing special about it, rows of binders, books on business, a few awards.

But Nate presses his hand against the side panel, firm, practiced.

A soft click echoes through the room.

The entire bookcase shifts an inch, then another, swinging open like a hidden door.

Behind it, only darkness.

Cold brushes down my spine. My breath stutters.

"Nate... what is that?"

He turns back to me with that same unreadable calm.

"A room," he says simply. "One you've earned the right to see."

I stare at the doorway, dread and curiosity twisting together in my stomach like two tangled vines.

I should walk away.

I should tell him no.

I should run.

But I don't.

Because the truth is terrifyingly simple, no matter how many warning bells ring in my chest, I want answers more.

And he knows it.

"Nate," I whisper, "why is it hidden?"

He steps aside, gesturing for me to come closer.

"You'll understand once you're inside."

My legs feel unsteady as I take a single step toward the doorway, toward the dark, the unknown, and whatever truth he's been keeping from me.

And the worst part?

Linine Langley

I'm not sure whether I'm walking into danger…

or finally uncovering the part of him I've always been drawn to.

***

The moment I step through the hidden doorway, the air changes. It's warmer, heavier, as though the room itself is holding its breath. Soft amber light glows from dozens of candles set along the walls, their flames flickering gently and casting long shadows across velvet drapes and deep-coloured furnishings. There's no violence here. No horror. But an intensity radiates from the space, purposeful and intimate, like walking straight into someone's private thoughts.

I swallow hard. My skin prickles with a mix of nerves and something harder to name.

Nate watches me quietly as I take it all in. He doesn't touch me, doesn't crowd me, he just lets me stand in the centre of the room while he closes the door behind us with a soft click.

"This," he says, voice low but steady, "is where I come when I want the truth."

The words settle over me like a weight. I turn to face him, my heart thumping so loudly I'm sure he can hear it.

"What… what is this place?" I manage.

He steps closer, slow and deliberate, until he's only a breath away. "A room built on trust. On honesty. On giving yourself without holding back."

My pulse jumps. "Nate, I don't understand."

He searches my face, his gaze deep enough to unsettle me. "You went through my things, Jane."

The sentence lands between us like a dropped stone.

I open my mouth to defend myself, but nothing comes out. The room, it does something to me. The lighting, the quiet, his calm certainty. It makes every word feel too loud, too flimsy.

Passionate Poison

Nate touches my jaw lightly, guiding my face up to his. Not forceful, just firm enough that I feel the expectation behind it.

"Tell me why."

I try again. "I... I wasn't trying to spy on you. I just... found something strange. The invoices. And then the drawer. It felt like something wasn't right."

His thumb brushes my cheek, slow and calculated. "So, you doubted me."

"I..." I hesitate. "I was confused."

He studies me with a look that feels like he's peeling back layers I didn't know I had. "Confusion is just fear wearing a prettier dress."

I breathe out shakily. He's right, in a way I hate to admit.

"Do you want the truth?" he asks.

"I thought I did," I whisper.

"And now?"

"I'm... not sure."

He gives a faint, knowing smile. "That's honest, at least."

He steps back slightly, giving me space, though somehow the distance feels even more consuming. "This room is for clarity, Jane. Not punishment. Not games. It's where nothing gets hidden, not from me, and not from yourself."

His voice drops, rich and warm. "But honesty goes both ways."

I stare at him, the uneasy swirl of fear and longing tightening in my chest. "So, what does that mean?"

"It means," he says, approaching me again, "that I'll show you everything you want to know... if you can look at me without flinching."

I feel the air catch in my throat. His closeness is overwhelming, heat and shadows and the scent of his skin pulling me deeper into something I don't fully understand.

"Nate," I murmur, "I don't want to lose myself."

His hand cups the back of my neck gently, guiding me just a little closer. "Then don't lose yourself. Trust yourself. Trust me."

"But that's the problem," I whisper back. "I don't know if trust is what this is… or if I'm just letting you in because I'm scared to lose you."

For a moment, he closes his eyes, like my honesty hits him somewhere he didn't expect. When he opens them again, they're softer, but still intense.

"Fear," he says, "is just another kind of desire."

I shouldn't feel drawn to that. I shouldn't feel the heat that moves through me when he says it. But I do. That's the part that terrifies me.

He lifts my hand and presses it to his chest. His heart is thudding hard beneath my palm. "You think I don't feel this too? You think you're the only one who's scared?"

I look up at him, startled. "Are you?"

"Of course, I am," he breathes. "You're under my skin, Jane. That's not easy for me."

My chest tightens. His honesty pulls at me, tugging the floor out from under all my doubts.

He leans in, his forehead resting against mine, the closeness dizzying. "But I can't build anything real with secrets between us. Not yours, not mine."

I whisper, "Then tell me what this room really means."

"It means," he murmurs, "that when you walk in here, you stop pretending. You stop running. You let yourself feel everything, good or bad."

A beat.

Passionate Poison

"And you let me in."

Heat pools low in my stomach, not physical heat, but emotional, raw and terrifying.

I whisper, "And what if I lose control?"

His fingers gently curl around mine. "Then I'll hold it for you."

A shiver runs through me. Not fear, exactly. Not desire alone. Something in between, something darker and more intimate than either.

I stand there in the candlelit hush, in a room built on secrets and truths I'm not sure I'm ready to hear, and realise I've crossed a line I can't uncross.

Because part of me wants to trust him completely.

And another part knows that trusting him might be the most dangerous thing I've ever done.

Either way, I'm in too deep to pretend otherwise.

Chapter Six:
Cracks in The Illusion

I've become very good at pretending.

Pretending I'm fine.

Pretending Nate and I are fine.

Pretending that what happened in that hidden room didn't shake something loose inside me.

I keep smiling, keep nodding, keep acting as though everything is exactly how he wants it to be. But beneath all that, I'm watching him. Every gesture. Every smooth apology. Every moment his charm slips just enough for me to glimpse the steel underneath.

I don't let him see that I've changed too.

That I'm no longer trusting, or naïve, or easy to soothe.

I'm studying him now, just as carefully as he's been studying me.

He thinks he knows me.

He thinks he owns me.

But he forgets I've lived too many lives, survived too many storms, to crumble so easily.

It's a funny thing, once you see darkness in someone, you start finding shadows everywhere.

Nate sits across from me at breakfast, sipping coffee like nothing in the world is wrong. He brushes his thumb across my wrist, soft and slow, the way he knows weakens my knees.

"Did you sleep well, baby doll?"

His voice is smooth, too smooth, and his eyes hold that quiet intensity that once thrilled me.

Now it unsettles me.

Passionate Poison

I smile like the perfect lover.

A mask I've become disturbingly good at wearing.

"Yes," I lie. "You?"

He leans in, kisses my cheek, lingers too long.

"I always sleep well when you're close."

Something cold ripples through me, but I make sure it doesn't show.

***

Monique arrives that afternoon, my safe place, my constant, my one person I thought I could always trust.

She practically throws her arms around me before she's even through the door.

"Oh, Jane… you look exhausted. What's going on?"

And just like that, my walls soften.

I let her in.

We sit on the lounge with wine, and I tell her pieces of the truth. Not everything. Not the parts I still can't name. But enough that she understands something is very wrong.

Or so I think.

Her eyes stay locked on mine the whole time, wide and concerned, but there's something else there too, something sharp, something glittering.

Curiosity?

Envy?

Hunger?

I can't place it. I'm too tired to try.

When I finally finish, she exhales slowly, almost theatrically.

"Jesus, Jane… that's heavy. Really heavy. And he acted like everything was normal after?"

"Too normal," I say quietly. "Like he was rehearsing it."

She bites her lip, thoughtful.

Too thoughtful.

"Well… maybe he's just scared of losing you."

The comment makes my skin prickle.

She says it too gently.

Too deliberately.

Almost defending him.

I force a laugh. "Scared? Nate doesn't get scared. He gets controlling."

She tilts her head. "Sometimes control is a sign someone just… really wants you."

Something in her tone is off.

But I'm slow to catch it. My mind is still caught in that room with Nate, his voice, his stare, the way he pushed every boundary I had until they weren't boundaries anymore.

***

But later, when I'm up getting another bottle of wine, I hear it, the slightest shift in her voice, soft but sharp:

"What was he wearing when he snapped like that?"

She asks it like she's asking about the weather.

But the question is too intimate.

Too hungry.

Too invested.

My stomach tightens.

Then another:

"Is he always that intense in the bedroom?"

She says it with faux innocence, swirling her wine like she's bored.

Passionate Poison

I turn slowly.

She meets my eyes with a smile that doesn't reach hers.

Not even close.

And suddenly… things click into place.

The way she's been watching me.

Watching him.

Asking about him.

Asking about us.

Piece by piece.

Layer by layer.

Like someone studying a puzzle she already intends to solve.

I swallow.

"You seem very interested, Mon."

She smirks, so faintly I almost miss it.

"Just curious, babe. You've always had the good stories."

But something cold creeps into my spine.

A warning.

A whisper.

Don't trust her.

Not this time.

***

Hours later, Nate calls. His voice is low, warm, intimate, dangerously familiar.

"How's your night, baby doll?"

Monique is in the kitchen. I lower my voice.

"Fine."

Linine Langley

He hums, that same sound he makes when he's pleased.

"You know I miss you... don't you?"

My breath catches.

Not because of his words, but because I notice it now.

The act.

The coaxing.

The control hidden beneath affection.

"Yes," I say softly.

Because what else can I say?

I hang up and turn.

Monique stands in the doorway, wine glass in hand, watching me.

Her smile is slow.

Measured.

Predatory.

"I can see why you're hooked," she murmurs.

My throat tightens.

Something is wrong.

Terribly wrong.

And I'm only just beginning to see it.

The cracks in the foundation aren't small anymore.

They're widening.

Between me and Nate.

Between me and Monique.

Between who I was... and who I'm becoming.

I sit down, feeling the weight of the world close around me.

Two dangerous people.

Passionate Poison

Two different intentions.

And I'm caught between them, bleeding trust on both sides.

I'm starting to realise the truth:

I might not be safe with Nate.

But I might be even less safe with her.

And the scariest part?

I can feel the storm coming,

and part of me is still drawn to the lightning.

***

I should have known something was off the moment Monique lingered at the doorway, hip leaned against the frame like she owned the place. But at the time I was exhausted, emotionally drained from the mess Nate and I had gotten ourselves tangled in, and her presence felt like relief. Familiar. Safe.

Or so I told myself.

She'd been around more than usual. Turning up after work with takeaway or a bottle of wine. Sitting a little too comfortably on Nate's couch. Laughing a little too loudly at jokes he didn't even make.

And the way she watched him…

That slow, measured glance up and down his body, like she was tasting him with her eyes.

I should have seen it.

But I didn't.

I was too busy trying to hold myself together.

One afternoon, she drifted into the office while I was sorting through the last of Nate's paperwork. She leaned over my shoulder, her breath warm on my neck as she said, "He's really something, isn't he?"

I didn't think anything of it then.

Linine Langley

Just Monique being blunt, as she always was.

Later that night, Nate and I had one of our usual arguments, short, sharp, stupid. Nothing dramatic. Just a clash of moods. He said I was withdrawing. I said he was controlling. Silence settled like dust, thick, choking, impossible to ignore.

I'd had enough for the night, so I went to bed early, still wearing the bitterness of the argument on my skin. Before closing the door, I heard the clink of wine glasses and Monique saying, *"I'll stay up with him, babe. Let you rest."*

I didn't think twice.

That was my mistake.

***

I lay in the dark, staring at the ceiling, listening to the murmur of voices drifting down the hallway. Low. Intimate. Too close.

At first, I told myself they were probably talking about work, or about me, Monique always liked to play mediator. But the tone of the conversation shifted. The pauses got longer. The silences thicker.

And then I heard it, that soft, velvety note in her voice she only used when she wanted something.

"Honestly, Nate... you've been carrying so much. Anyone would snap under that pressure."

A quiet hum from him.

Agreement.

Openness.

She was sliding in under his guard like warm honey.

"I just... want you to know you deserve better than constant drama," she continued, her voice dripping sympathy. "You're loyal. You're passionate. You give everything."

A pause.

Passionate Poison

Then, softly:

"Does Jane even appreciate how much you do?"

My stomach twisted.

A creeping cold spread through me.

I sat up in bed, but I couldn't move, like my own body didn't want me to hear any more.

Their voices lowered again, dipping to a whisper. I strained to catch the rhythm of it, not the words, the rhythm was enough.

Monique's laugh floated down the hallway, warm and low.

The kind of laugh she used when she was letting someone know they had her full attention.

The kind of laugh men always fell for.

The kind Nate was falling for right now.

I heard footsteps.

Soft.

Slow.

Measured.

Then another set.

Heavier.

Following.

Not towards me.

Away from me.

Towards the living room.

My heart rammed against my ribs.

Something was happening out there.

Something I didn't want to picture but couldn't stop imagining.

Their voices faded into something… breathier. Pauses stretched. The air seemed to thicken even from where I sat, as though I could feel the heat of their bodies through the walls.

Monique had always been bold. Sensual. Dangerous in the way only women who know their power can be.

And Nate…

He thrived on being wanted. Needed. Admired.

God.

I could feel it happening.

Even without seeing a thing.

The way the room seemed to pulse with a different kind of energy, something forbidden, something hot enough to sear.

The way the silence between their murmurs curled around me like smoke.

The way my skin prickled, not from jealousy alone but from the knowledge that a line, a massive, life-altering, relationship-ruining line, was being crossed several metres away.

I sat there, frozen, barely breathing, as a muffled sound floated down the hall.

A soft gasp, not pain, not surprise, something else entirely.

Something unmistakably intimate.

Something that didn't belong to me.

My chest tightened until it hurt.

I pressed a hand over my mouth to stop the sob building there.

Nate's voice came next, low, rough, the sound I knew too well. The sound he made when he forgot himself.

I curled into myself, shaking.

Not from the betrayal, not entirely.

Passionate Poison

But from the realisation that parts of him he'd reserved for me...

he was giving to her.

Monique.

My oldest friend.

My closest confidant.

My safe place.

She was doing this.

With him.

Behind my back.

Under my roof.

The sound of a wineglass knocking against a table drifted through the wall. A hushed moan followed, full-bodied, breathless, swallowed quickly but not quickly enough.

I pressed both hands against my ears, but it didn't matter.

I could feel the betrayal.

Taste it.

Hear it in the air.

Sense it in the rhythm of their movements.

Nate wasn't resisting her.

He wasn't pushing her away.

He wasn't even hesitating.

They were giving in to something raw and reckless, something fuelled by lust, adrenaline, ego, and the thrill of the forbidden.

And I...

I was lying in bed like a ghost.

An observer to the destruction of my own life.

Linine Langley

Every breath felt like swallowing glass.

Every second stretched like a punishment.

By the time silence finally settled again, thick, spent, satisfied, I wasn't the same woman who'd closed her bedroom door hours earlier.

I'd felt the crack happen.

Right down my centre.

Clean.

Sharp.

Irreversible.

And I knew, without doubt, that nothing between the three of us would ever be the same again.

***

Morning crawls in slow and pale, the kind of light that feels neither warm nor welcome. I open my eyes and know instantly something is wrong. The air feels thick, charged, like a storm has passed through while I slept.

I sit up, rubbing my temples, trying to remember what time I went to bed. I'd been upset, drained, barely able to keep my eyes open. I only vaguely recall Monique pouring another glass of wine... her voice floating in the hallway... Nate's low laugh...

I thought they were just talking.

God, how stupid am I.

When I step out into the kitchen, they're both there.

And everything inside me drops.

Nate is standing by the counter, polite smile plastered on his face like it's been pinned there. Monique is leaning against the breakfast bar with a friendliness so sugary it could rot teeth. They both turn to look at me, and though they're smiling, something in the air snaps tight around my ribs.

Passionate Poison

"Morning, gorgeous," Nate says, voice too bright, too smooth.

Monique's smile widens. "Hey, babe, you look exhausted. Rough night?"

Her eyes flicker, just for a split second, toward Nate.

It's quick. Too quick for anyone else to notice.

But I see it.

A silent pulse of something hot and forbidden between them.

My heart doesn't drop. It slams.

I pretend not to notice. I pretend too well.

I move through the kitchen like I'm underwater, picking up on details I shouldn't be noticing but can't stop seeing:

A glass on the bench that wasn't there last night, lipstick on the rim, not my shade.

A soft, floral perfume lingering in the air, Monique's, too close, too strong.

A towel thrown over the back of a chair, still damp, not mine.

Nate's eyes avoid mine, then cling too tightly, then avoid again. No middle ground. No ease. Just guilt wearing charm like a badly fitted suit.

And Monique…

Monique can't stop smiling.

But it's the wrong smile.

Too polished.

Too controlled.

Too careful.

She keeps reaching out, touching my arm, brushing my hair back, fussing like she's the world's most devoted friend.

But her hands shake.

Linine Langley

She tries to hide it, but I see.

My stomach twists so sharply I have to grip the bench.

I don't know what happened.

Not properly.

Not clearly.

But I can feel it.

The betrayal sits in the air like smoke, heavy, hot, impossible to breathe around.

Nate clears his throat, his voice low. "Got an early call, girl. Might have to head in."

He won't look at me when he says it.

Not properly.

Not the way he always does.

Monique straightens, grabs her bag quickly, too quickly.

"Yeah, I should go too," she blurts out, avoiding his gaze, avoiding mine. "Didn't realise the time."

Her hug is all wrong.

It feels staged.

Her body is stiff, her breath uneven.

"Love you," she whispers into my hair.

But the words slide over me like cold oil.

Wrong.

Forced.

Contaminated.

She pulls back, eyes glassy. "We'll catch up later, yeah?"

I nod, though every part of me screams no.

Passionate Poison

She turns away, and I swear for one second, just one, her face shatters. Guilt. Desire. Triumph. Something feral. Something broken.

Then she's gone.

The door closes softly, but it hits me like a slammed gate.

Nate steps closer, palm brushing down my arm with a tenderness that should soothe me. It doesn't. It burns.

"You, okay?" he asks softly.

The gentleness in his voice feels like a lie wrapped in silk.

I swallow hard. "Yeah. Just tired."

He nods slowly, eyes searching mine, too intensely, too carefully, like he's checking whether I've seen through him.

The moment stretches between us, full of heat, fear, and a strange ache that feels dangerously close to grief.

He kisses my forehead, longer than usual. "I'll make it up to you later, girl."

I nod, because I can't trust my voice.

He leaves.

The house goes silent.

Completely silent.

And then the truth, or some shadow of it, wraps around me like ice.

I sink into the chair, gripping the edge of the table as if the world is tilting.

Something happened.

I know it.

I feel it down to the bone.

Something sweet turned sour in the night.

Something intimate slipped out of my hands.

Linine Langley

Something warm between us has curdled into something sharp.

I whisper into the emptiness, voice barely a breath:

"Something's wrong.

Something's very, very wrong."

And even though I don't know the details…

I can taste the betrayal like heat on the back of my tongue,

seductive, poisonous, and unmistakably real.

Chapter Seven:
I Have Lost All Trust

The next day Nate left some peculiar gifts for me, they accompanied a detailed note, a sort of guide to my own demise. I did what he told me to do. I slid into the black lace dress Nate had picked out, impossibly tight, the kind that felt more like an idea than fabric, and buckled the Louboutins on like armour. The bra he chose left little to the imagination; for once I went my own way and slipped on a tiny black G-string beneath it. It felt like a small rebellion. Not loud enough to matter, but mine all the same.

I finished my make-up slow and careful. A dab of foundation, a sweep of brown shadow to make my eyes look deep, black mascara, and a red lip that wasn't so red it screamed. I pulled my hair out and let it sit in soft waves. I practised the right smile in the bathroom mirror, the one that said I was composed, that I had nothing to hide. Then I told myself the lie long enough to believe it for the walk across the room.

When he came in, he stood just inside the doorway, taking me in like he was inspecting a prize. He didn't touch me at first. He watched. There was hunger in the way his eyes moved, possessiveness coiled behind the look, and then, a subtle shift, something calculating that made my skin prick.

"You look perfect," he said, voice low. "Absolutely perfect." He took a breath as though savouring me, and then, as if remembering his place in whatever play he was conducting, he smiled and stepped forward to kiss my cheek. The kiss was warm, public, practiced. I felt the press of his palm on the small of my back guiding me toward the car. I did what I'd learned to do: I let him lead.

The restaurant was all polished wood and low lighting, candles flickering like small confessions. People eased into their meals and into the kind of conversation that keeps strangers warm and couples safe. Nate smiled and charmed and ordered. He was the partner everyone wanted, interested, witty, in control. He brushed my hand under the table once, then my thigh, small touches given like proof of ownership. On the surface, we were an item in the way the world understands it: beautiful, enviable, uncomplicated.

But the touch felt staged. Rehearsed. I caught the tiniest staccato of movement in his jaw when the waiter took the wine away, like an actor waiting for the right cue. My stomach tightened, a small animal in my ribs sensing danger before the mind knew the shape of it.

I excused myself to the loo, a reasonable little lie: lipstick touch-up, a moment to breathe. The corridor felt far too quiet. When I slipped into the dim washroom and closed the door, my hands were shaking a little, not from the heels but from the weight of waiting.

Through the cracked door I saw him, crouched slightly, his head bent, one hand braced against the wall, the glow from his phone flickering over his face. He wasn't laughing, not exactly, but his whole posture was intimate, private. I couldn't hear the words at first; the restaurant's hum swallowed them. Then a low, familiar softness reached me, a line of a sentence I'd heard only in the safest hours, the hours when we'd let down our guards and told each other inconvenient truths.

"See you soon, darling," he murmured.

The word landed on me like ice. Darling. The way he said it, the crease at the corner of his mouth, the soft cadence, it was the same part of him that had once been mine. The one that had held me when things felt impossibly raw. It sounded like the echo of a promise. But this time it wasn't mine.

For a second, I considered barging out, throwing the door open and asking, demanding, poisoning the evening with my truth. I could picture the scene: the waiter stunned, the heads turning, Nate's expression folding like a map being crushed. But some part of me, the part that still kept a ledger of what might ruin us, stayed my hand. I smoothed my dress instead, practised calm, and went back to the table with a smile nailed into place.

He pulled my chair out for me with a gentleman's flourish, kissed my shoulder, and whispered, "You look good enough to devour." His

Passionate Poison

hands were warm on my back, and I felt that old, dangerous pull: the chemistry I couldn't deny, the way he could make my pulse do things I barely had words for. It made everything more confusing. It made everything more dangerous.

I sipped my wine and tried to read him in the reflection on the glass. He laughed at my jokes, leaned in as though he wanted to share secrets, and then leaned away when the music changed. His eyes met mine and for a moment they were the man I thought I loved. Then they flicked, brief and precise, to the doorway like a guard checking a horizon.

My intuition is a blunt instrument sometimes. Tonight, it felt surgical. He wants me distracted, I thought. He wants me compliant. He can't have me looking too closely. He needs me pliable. The idea made me feel like a marionette watched by fingers behind the curtains.

Was he dangerous? Or was I the one fraying at the edges, losing my grip on what was real? The doubt arrived like a taste at the back of my mouth, bitter and metallic.

By the time dessert came, Nate's hand found mine again with the tenderness of a man who says all the right words. He kissed the back of my wrist and mouthed something I couldn't quite catch. I returned the gesture because it was the currency we traded: small intimacies for the illusion of security.

On the drive home, he took my hand between both of his, thumb rubbing a slow circle on the inside of my wrist. "I'll show you how much you mean to me," he murmured. I wanted to lean in, to let the warmth wash the cold away, but when I looked at him in the rear-view mirror his eyes were guarded, and that calculation was back again. He seemed to hold two people in his face: the man who looked like my lover, and the man who is practised at wearing other faces.

At home I stood in the dim hall and listened for the sound of his breathing. I told myself that love warps things, that men are complicated, that perhaps I was paranoid because I had been hurt before. Then I replayed him on the phone, the word *darling* like a secret whistle, and the certainty of betrayal tightened like a glove around my throat.

I lay awake that night, heels tucked by the bed, the black dress still warm from the night. The house hummed with the invisible work of cleaning up after our performance: the scent of his cologne, the faint sugar on my lips, the image of him folding himself back into composure.

The mask slips sometimes. I can see it now, a crack along the veneer, a tiny fissure that grows under pressure. Monique is loose at the edges, too, I see her in the way she watches him, the way she smiles at me with a softness that feels like a dare. I tell myself the paranoia is mine. I tell myself to trust the man who says he loves me.

And yet, as I drift toward sleep, I realise I no longer know which version of him I am waking up to, the man who holds me sacred, or the one who will say *darling* to someone else and still smile into my face.

***

Monique starts appearing the way a storm rolls in—slow at first, then suddenly everywhere.

At first, it's subtle. A text:

"Hey babe, you home? Thought I'd drop in for a cuppa."

Then another.

Then a knock at the door even when I haven't answered the messages.

She breezes in like she owns the place, like she's checking the temperature of the air between Nate and me. She's all warm smiles and soft hugs, hair perfectly messy, perfume thick enough to cling to the curtains.

Nate pretends he's barely noticed her… but I *see* him notice.

A flick of his eyes.

A shift in his breathing.

Passionate Poison

A pause too long.

It's microscopic, but it hits me like a punch.

I tell myself I'm imagining it.

I tell myself I'm tired.

I tell myself trauma makes shadows where none exist.

But then Monique starts saying things.

Not outright.

Not enough to accuse her.

Just enough to make my skin crawl.

"God, Nate's such a strong man," she says once, leaning on the kitchen bench like she's posing for a camera.

Another day, she's swirling wine in her glass, eyes drifting to where he sits.

"You're lucky, Jane. Not many men know exactly what they want."

Exactly. What. They. Want.

Each syllable drips like honey turned sour.

Nate smirks at the comment, pretending he's laughing at something else entirely.

He doesn't correct her.

He doesn't look at me.

He lets it hang in the air.

And that's when something shifts sharply inside me—something I don't have a name for.

***

It starts small.

The undermining.

Linine Langley

Whenever Monique is around, Nate becomes sweeter to me… and somehow crueler.

Not in words.

In tone.

In the way he says, "Jane gets a bit emotional sometimes," like he's patting a child on the head.

Or, "She overthinks things—don't you, baby?"

said with a smile that doesn't reach his eyes.

Monique nods solemnly, as if she's my therapist.

My heart thuds so loudly I'm certain they can hear it.

I force a laugh, make some joke, try to keep the peace.

But I feel it.

I feel the shift.

Like I've slipped out of the centre of something I didn't know I was balancing.

***

They start exchanging glances when they think I'm not looking.

Fast, sharp, electric glances.

Glances that say:

I know something you don't.

And suddenly I'm the outsider in my own home.

One night Nate snaps at me for something tiny—me forgetting to take chicken out of the freezer, of all things. He storms out to the balcony, calling it "getting some air."

Monique touches my shoulder gently.

"Babe, don't take it personally. He just needs space."

Passionate Poison

But instead of going home, she wanders toward the hallway where Nate is, her steps slow, deliberate.

She stops outside his closed door and just… stands there.

I watch her profile silhouetted in the dim light, the shape of her breath slowing, deepening, almost as if she's listening to *him* breathe on the other side.

A slow, thick heat coils in the room.

Fear.

Jealousy.

Recognition.

I swallow hard and pretend I didn't notice.

***

Later that night I hear something—a muted gasp, soft as fabric sliding against skin.

I freeze in bed, heart in my throat.

I wait.

Silence.

Then another sound, barely there, like someone catching breath too quickly.

I get up, creep to the hallway.

The house is dark, still, impossibly quiet.

Too quiet.

When I walk into the living room, everything is perfectly placed.

Pristine.

Innocent.

Except…

A wine glass that wasn't there earlier.

Linine Langley

A cushion dented on the wrong side of the couch.

A faint scent in the air—warm, earthy, and not mine.

When I turn, Nate is coming from the opposite end of the house.

His shirt is buttoned wrong.

He's out of breath.

"Thought you were asleep," he says casually, rubbing the back of his neck.

"Thought you were," I answer.

We stand staring at each other, the air thick enough to choke on.

Before I can ask anything, he crosses the room, kisses my forehead, murmurs something about "late-night thinking" and "needing clarity."

But his eyes keep darting toward the hallway where Monique had stood earlier.

I know I'm being played.

I don't have proof.

But I know.

***

The days that follow are slow torture.

Nate acts extra patient, extra affectionate, extra everything.

It's the kind of affection that feels like being wrapped in silk… while your wrists are quietly tied behind your back.

Monique pops by again and again.

Her smile is bright enough to blind.

Her hugs last too long.

She compliments him.

She compliments me.

But behind her eyes is something hungry.

Passionate Poison

Something territorial.

Something I don't want to recognise.

At one point Nate walks past her and their fingers brush ever so slightly.

Not enough to call accidental.

Not enough to prove intentional.

Just enough to split me open inside.

I go still.

Cold.

Numb.

They both pretend nothing happened.

I pretend I didn't notice.

That night, as I lie awake staring at the ceiling, a horrible truth takes shape slowly, painfully, undeniably:

There's three of us in this relationship.

And I'm the only one who doesn't know the rules.

***

The morning was wrong before I even opened my eyes. There was a weight in the house that didn't belong to me, heavy and silent and impossible to ignore. I lay there for a few moments, listening for the small, everyday noises that usually made me feel safe: the kettle clicking, Nate's shower, the soft shuffle of a day beginning. Instead, there was a peculiar stillness, like the house was holding its breath.

When I pushed the doona back and swung my legs over the side of the bed, Nate wasn't beside me. That should have been ordinary, he often beat me up for a run or slid out for a call, but today his absence felt pointed, like the missing piece of something I hadn't known was whole. I padded across the hall and heard the shower already running, long and steady. He sings under the water when he's relaxed; this was nothing like that. The rhythm felt forced, the sort of vigorous rinsing one does to erase more than salt.

I came into the living room wrapped in my robe and everything hit me at once. Monique's perfume was there, a faint ghost of jasmine and something darker. It clung to the curtains, to the arm of the couch, like a lingering breath. I hadn't noticed her wearing it last night when she'd come over for what she said would be a quick catch-up. I hadn't thought to notice because I hadn't wanted to look too closely.

A wine glass sat on the coffee table, lipstick ghosting the rim. A cushion was pushed askew as if someone had taken a breath too deep on it and left in a hurry. A towel lay in a crumpled heap by the laundry door, damp at one corner. Little domestic things, all of them, but entirely out of place. None of them were evidence on their own. Together they were a map pointing to a truth I could feel but wouldn't yet name.

I stood there, hands tucked into my robe, pretending not to notice, trying to catch my breath like a criminal who knows she's been seen but is hoping she misread the glance. The rational part of me, the part that'd built careers out of order and boundaries, told me not to jump. Don't be ridiculous, it said. People leave towels. People forget glasses. Perfume is nothing. But the rest of me, the part that's kept a tally of small silences and diverted gazes, tightened. My skin prickled in a way that no argument could soothe.

Nate emerged from the bathroom fifteen minutes later, hair damp, towel slung over his shoulder. He smiled at me, that smile he gives that usually melts something soft inside my chest, and stepped forward as if to kiss me. I flinched instead. He seemed startled by it and then terribly conciliatory. He smoothed the robe at my shoulders, ran a hand along my arm, and said, all sweetness and easy charm, "Rough night, baby doll? You look tired."

His fingers lingered, but there was no hunger to them. They were ministrations, not the quick claiming touch he sometimes used. It was as if he was trying to sew over something that had frayed. He kissed my forehead as if to prove that closeness, then stepped back and busied

Passionate Poison

himself with making coffee. He hummed the way he does when he's trying to keep the mood neutral. It read like guilt.

Monique appeared from the kitchen with an exaggerated brightness, a cheery "Morning, beautiful!" that didn't meet my eyes properly. Her hug was tight, a little too calculated. She pressed her cheek to mine and lingered, breathing that perfume across my skin. It should have been comforting, friends are meant to smell like other people sometimes, but the contact felt like a message. Her grip said, *I was here.* Her eyes flicked to Nate and back to me with an odd hesitation that I didn't understand, and I felt the first real, sharp twist of betrayal.

She made a show of being helpful, clearing the wine glass, folding the towel, smoothing the cushion as if she were tidying up an accident. "I've got to dash early today," she announced suddenly, too brightly. "Something's come up." Her voice hit a notch higher than necessary, the kind of voice people use when they're nervous and invent cheerfulness to hide it. Her goodbye hug felt like the last act in a play, perfectly rehearsed, too long by half. She kept my face in her hands for a second, then stepped back sharply, avoided my eyes, and left.

The second she was gone, Nate's manner shifted again. He moved closer, closed the distance that had been conspicuously polite that morning. He touched my neck, murmured something about how I looked incredible in the dress he'd chosen. His words were honeyed, intimate. But the heat they usually sparked in me was a task I couldn't summon. Instead, there was a nausea made of awareness. His hands were deft, tender almost, but his eyes flicked past me to the doorway where Monique had stood. He kissed me with a precision that read like an apology and a calculation.

He tried to erase the morning with affection, an overcompensation that felt like an attempt to re-write a page that had already been torn out. He spoke soft promises: *You're my girl. You're the one I want.* He used phrases that once felt like anchors. They felt now like varnish applied over rot.

I moved through the day gutted by a thousand small trebles: a missed glance, a too-eager compliment from Monique when she texted later, the faint scent of jasmine clinging to the collar of the shirt Nate left on a chair. My phone buzzed with a message from Monique, *Sorry couldn't stay longer, love you,* three small words that felt like a closed door.

That night I lay in bed and pressed my palms to my temples until the throb slowed. I whispered into the darkness, more to steady myself than to expect an answer, "Something's wrong. Something's very, very wrong."

The whisper was a small, simple thing, but it felt like truth. The kind of truth that doesn't need proof to exist, the slow, certain knowledge that something had shifted irreparably in the room I thought I owned. And while I listened for an answer, I understood with dreadful clarity that the answer might not arrive from them at all. It would have to come from me.

Chapter Eight: The Hard Way

I knew something was wrong with me long before I admitted it out loud.

It started as a tightness in my chest, the kind you get when you're anxious or overtired. But mine didn't go away. It tightened, then eased, then tightened again like some invisible hand was squeezing the air out of my lungs just to see how far I'd bend before I snapped.

I told myself it was stress.

I told myself it was lack of sleep.

I told myself it was Nate.

I told myself every excuse except the truth.

By mid-morning I could barely stand. My legs shook, my vision blurred around the edges. My head felt stuffed with cotton, heavy and slow, like I was thinking through fog. And yet, I'd never been more awake. My heart wouldn't stop racing, a wild skittering rhythm that scared me more than I wanted to admit.

Nate noticed immediately.

Or maybe he'd been waiting for it.

"You look pale, baby doll," he said, sliding a glass into my hand. "Drink this. You just need to relax."

Relax.

The word scraped against my nerves like sandpaper.

The drink tasted... wrong.

A bitter echo I didn't recognise, something chemical sitting underneath the sweetness. I forced a smile, pretended I didn't taste it at all, and placed the glass down the moment he turned his back.

Within minutes, the room began to tilt.

Linine Langley

By the afternoon I couldn't breathe properly. My chest felt tight, sharp, almost bruised. I tried to tell Nate I needed help, but he only stroked my cheek and murmured, "You're fine. Just sit down. You always panic."

But I wasn't panicking.

My body was failing.

When my knees buckled, he caught me, not with concern, but irritation, as if I'd interrupted his plans.

"For fuck's sake, Jane," he muttered, hauling me upright. "Come on. I'll take you to the hospital. Christ, you're a mess."

His words sliced through me sharper than the pain in my chest.

He didn't rush.

He didn't shout for help.

He didn't show fear.

He just guided me to the car like he was ticking a chore off his list.

By the time we got to Emergency, my vision was flickering, black, light, black again. Nurses took one look at me and rushed over with a wheelchair. Nate stayed behind, arms folded, jaw clenched, looking more annoyed than worried.

They wheeled me into a curtained bay, slapped leads on my chest, took blood, pushed a needle into my arm. Everything felt distant. Muffled. Like I was underwater and the world was happening above the surface.

A doctor appeared, a middle-aged woman with steady eyes and hands that didn't shake when she touched my wrist.

"Jane, love, your heart rate is through the roof. Has this happened before?"

"No," I whispered. "I… I don't know what's happening to me."

She exchanged a look with the nurse beside her. A look that made my stomach drop.

Passionate Poison

"We're keeping you for observation. Your tests show irregular heart activity and signs of chemical interference."

"Interference?" I asked, breath hitching. "What does that mean?"

Before she could answer, Nate pushed the curtain aside.

Too calm.

Too controlled.

"How is she?" he asked, in a voice that didn't belong to the man I loved. "She'll be fine, won't she? Probably just worn out."

The doctor stiffened. "Sir, we need to run a few more tests. Could you wait outside?"

"I'm staying," Nate said, stepping closer to my bed.

Everything in me recoiled.

"Please," I whispered. "Nate... I just want to rest. Let me talk to the doctor alone."

His jaw tightened. For a moment I thought he'd argue. But then, with a forced smile and a cold pat on my leg, he said, "Of course, baby doll. I'll be right outside."

When he left, the doctor drew the curtain fully closed and lowered her voice.

"Jane, I need you to listen carefully. Your bloodwork shows traces of a sedative. Not one we typically prescribe. This one is... stronger."

The room seemed to tilt again.

"A sedative?" I repeated. "I, I don't take anything."

"I know," she said gently. "That's why I'm telling you now. Someone has been giving it to you without your knowledge. It's highly addictive. And dangerous to the heart."

My breath caught. My pulse hammered like it wanted out of my chest.

Dangerous to the heart.

Linine Langley

Every drink.

Every time he insisted.

Every night I felt too calm. Too sleepy. Too obedient.

Suddenly, everything made sense.

The dizziness.

The fog.

The lapses in memory.

The way he always had the remedy before I felt the sickness.

Nate didn't love me.

Nate was managing me.

A slow, cold terror spread through my body.

"Do you... do you know how long it's been in my system?" I asked.

She tapped the paper in her hand. "Long enough to explain the symptoms you're describing. We need to keep you in for a few days."

A few days.

Away from him.

Safe.

I nodded, tears burning behind my eyes, not from sadness, but from the shock of finally seeing the shape of the trap I'd walked into.

When the doctor stepped away, I stared at the ceiling, my throat tight, my heart pounding unevenly beneath my ribs.

The truth wasn't whispered.

It wasn't hidden.

It wasn't gentle.

It was chemical.

It was lethal.

Passionate Poison

And it had been inside me all along.

***

I hear the door open before I see her. At first, I think it's another nurse doing the usual checks, but when I turn my head, it's Monique, standing in the doorway like she's forgotten how to breathe. Her mascara is smudged, her hair looks like she's been running her hands through it for hours, and her shoulders are curved inward like she's trying to fold herself up.

For the first time since I've known her, she doesn't look seductive or confident.

She looks… wrecked.

"Mon…" My voice cracks. "What are you doing here?"

She shuts the door behind her and leans against it for a second, as if she needs it to stay upright. When she moves toward the bed, I can see her hands shaking. She sits down in the chair beside me and lets out a shaky breath.

"I have to tell you something," she whispers.

My stomach twists. After everything, the weird looks, the off comments, the nights Nate went "missing", I already know whatever she's about to say is going to rip something open.

"Jane… Nate and I,"

She swallows hard.

"We've been sleeping together."

Even though I knew, even though every instinct in my body has been screaming it, the words still cut like a blade. They slice through my chest, right under my ribs, sharp and cold.

For a moment I can't speak. I just stare at her.

Not because of the betrayal.

But because she looks so… sorry.

Linine Langley

She isn't hiding behind a smirk.

She isn't gearing up for a fight.

She's breaking apart.

"I'm not going to make excuses," she says, voice trembling. "I wanted him. I won't lie to you about that. I was stupid and selfish and... blinded."

I squeeze the blanket in my hands, trying to ground myself. The room feels too bright, too still.

"But Jane," She leans closer, her voice dropping. "There's something you don't know."

I take a breath, preparing myself for impact.

"Last night," she says, "Nate made me a drink. He said it was just something to help me relax. But when he walked away... I saw him slip something into it."

My blood runs cold.

"I pretended to drink it," she continues. "Tipped it into my sleeve when he wasn't looking." Her voice cracks. "I didn't know what it was, but something in me, something, told me not to trust him."

My heart thuds painfully. I think of the bitter taste in the drink he gave me. The dizziness. The collapsing.

"He went to bed thinking I'd had it," she whispers. "And later, when he thought I was asleep, he got on the phone."

My breath catches.

"Who was he talking to?"

"A girl named Laura." Monique's jaw tightens. "She sounded young. Too young."

A chill washes over me, spreading through my entire body.

"And Jane... he spoke to her the way he spoke to you."

Her voice is barely audible now.

Passionate Poison

"The exact same words."

I close my eyes as she continues:

"He told her she was beautiful, special. That he'd never met anyone like her. That he trusted her. That she belonged to him."

My chest feels like it's caving in.

Those lines, those exact lines, were once whispered against my skin, my neck, my mouth.

"He promised he'd take care of her," Monique adds quietly. "Said he'd show her 'a world she'd never forget.'"

The room spins. I steady myself against the mattress, fighting nausea.

"Jane…" Monique's voice shakes. "He's running the same script on all of us."

I can't breathe.

I can't think.

All I can feel is the walls closing in.

I tell her what the doctor said.

The drug.

The danger.

The manipulation.

The addiction.

Monique goes pale, covering her mouth with her hand.

"That, that stuff was in your system?" she whispers.

"Yes."

"And it's dangerous for the heart?"

"Yes."

"Jane…" She leans back, terrified. "He tried to give me that. If I had drunk it,"

Her voice splinters.

We sit in silence, both of us trembling.

She finally whispers, "We're not special. We were never special. We're not loved. We're…"

Her voice breaks completely.

"We're experiments."

I swallow hard, tears burning my eyes.

All those nights I thought I was losing my mind…

All those moments I thought I was paranoid, dramatic, crazy…

All those times Nate said I was "emotional," "overthinking," "too sensitive."

It was all real.

Every instinct.

Every warning.

Every ache in my chest.

"Laura…" I murmur. "She has no idea."

Monique shakes her head, wiping her eyes. "None."

For the first time since she walked in, she reaches for my hand. Tentatively. Like she expects me to pull away.

I don't.

Because underneath the betrayal and the anger and the heartbreak, there's something stronger, something sharper.

Fury.

Not at her.

Not anymore.

At him.

Passionate Poison

"We can't let him keep doing this," Monique whispers. "Not to you. Not to me. And not to her."

I nod slowly, breathing through the pain, through the betrayal, through the rising clarity.

"We're going to stop him," I say, my voice steady for the first time in days.

Monique squeezes my hand.

And in that hospital room, battered, bruised, drugged, betrayed, the two women he played against each other finally align.

Not as rivals.

Not as victims.

But as a storm he never saw coming.

***

The room is dim, lit only by the thin strip of light sneaking under the door. Machines hum softly around me, each beep a reminder of how close I came to disappearing. I sit upright against the pillows, my chest still tight, but my mind sharper than it's been in months.

Monique sits curled in the chair beside me, knees drawn up, arms wrapped around herself like she's holding in the truth so it doesn't tear her open. Not long ago, I thought she was my greatest betrayal. Now she looks like a woman who's seen the mask ripped off the devil.

"We need to start from the beginning," I whisper. "Everything we know."

She nods, eyes red but hardening. "Everything."

We talk quietly, almost afraid the walls might listen.

Piece by piece, we line up the horrors:

The secret room hidden behind Nate's bookcase.

The invoices from unknown women.

The flowers turning up at houses not mine.

Linine Langley

The private phone calls.

The drug, God, the drug, running through my veins like poison wearing a silk dress.

Laura.

The way he whispered to her like she was the only one he'd ever wanted.

It hits me then: his power was never emotional. He never broke my strong edges with love.

He used chemistry.

Sedation masked as tenderness.

Control disguised as passion.

I was so sure the ache in my chest was desire.

Turns out it was my heart fighting for its life.

Monique breathes out, slow and shaky. "He didn't love any of us."

"No," I say. "He studied us."

She flinches. "I thought... I don't know. I thought I had something over you. Something he wanted more. I was stupid."

"You weren't stupid," I tell her quietly. "You were targeted."

She looks up at me with eyes that are suddenly, startlingly honest. "So were you."

There's a strange connection between us now, built not from lust or rivalry, but from surviving the same storm. A shared wound. A shared fury.

And an urge I didn't expect:

To protect her.

To protect Laura.

To protect anyone else he's got lined up next.

Passionate Poison

"Jane," Monique whispers, "he tried to drug me. I saw him put something in the drink. If I'd taken it... I don't know what would've happened."

"He would've owned you," I whisper. "The same way he owned me."

Silence falls between us like a heavy curtain.

Then she straightens, jaw tightening the way it does when she's about to throw herself into trouble. "We can't let him keep doing this."

"No," I agree. "We can't."

"He deserves to be destroyed."

"And he will be," I say. "But we do it smart. We do it quietly. We do it right."

Monique leans in, voice trembling but fierce. "We protect Laura first."

"Yes."

"Then we gather evidence."

"Yes."

"And then," she breathes, "we ruin him."

A small, cold smile touches my lips. My body may be weak, but my mind is awake in a way it hasn't been for a long time. Nate gave me poison, but now I have clarity, sharp and dangerous.

And if he thinks I'm still the woman lying obediently in silk sheets, he has no idea what's coming.

Monique wipes her eyes. "I thought I was competing with you. Turns out we were both competing with a monster."

"No more competing," I say. "We're done playing by his rules."

The door handle clicks softly, and for a moment, both of us go still. My pulse spikes.

A nurse steps inside, smiling gently.

"There's a man outside," she says. "Nate. He wants to come in."

Linine Langley

My stomach drops.

Monique grips my wrist.

The nurse waits.

And something inside me, something that's been asleep ever since Nate touched my skin for the first time, finally wakes up. Strength. Rage. Self-preservation. I don't hesitate.

"Don't let him in," I say.

The nurse nods and leaves, closing the door behind her.

For the first time since this nightmare began, Nate is on the other side of a barrier he can't charm his way through. He can't touch me. Can't drug me. Can't whisper lies into my hair.

Monique lets out a long, shaking breath. "What now?"

I look at the closed door.

At the shadows.

At my bruised trust.

And at the needle marks on my arm that tell me exactly what I escaped.

"Now," I say softly, "we do it the hard way."

She nods, understanding.

Because there's only one way to take down a man like Nate:

Not with fear.

Not with longing.

Not with the softness he once pretended to love.

But with precision.

With truth.

With fury sharpened into strategy.

Monique reaches for my hand, and I let her take it.

"No more secrets," she whispers.

Passionate Poison

"No more," I promise.

And somewhere out in the corridor, Nate waits, smiling at a nurse, acting patient, pretending concern.

He has no idea the women he thought he broke are already rebuilding themselves into weapons.

For the first time, the power is shifting.

And he won't see the next move coming.

Linine Langley

Chapter Nine: Three Can Play the Game

I was still hooked up to half a dozen machines when Monique told me she needed "fresh air."

That was a lie.

I knew her well enough to recognise the look in her eyes, sharp, restless, itching for a target. She wanted to *do* something. Punch something. Or someone. And I already knew who that someone was.

Nate.

But he wasn't here to tear into, so Monique did the next best thing: she went looking for the newest girl in his twisted rotation, Laura. The one he'd whispered sweet lies to while Monique pretended to sleep. The one he'd called *darling* with the same voice he once saved for me.

Hours later, when Monique told me what she'd done, she struggled to hold her expression steady.

"This isn't what I expected," she whispered.

That's where the story begins.

***

Monique told me she drove across town with her heart pounding, half-sick with fury. She didn't even knock politely, she hammered on Laura's door as though she meant to break the thing clean off its hinges.

When the door finally opened, Monique froze.

Laura didn't look anything like the fragile little thing Nate had described. She wasn't teary, flustered, or doe-eyed. She stood tall and still, her expression steady, her dark hair tied back like she'd been waiting, not for company, but for a moment like this.

"Can I help you?" she asked, cool as anything.

Monique, already on edge, went straight for the throat.

Passionate Poison

"Yeah, you can. You can stop trying to seduce someone else's man."

Laura didn't blink.

Didn't flinch.

Didn't even pretend to misunderstand.

Instead she leaned her shoulder casually against the doorframe.

"I'm not here to seduce him," she said. "And he's not your man."

Monique bristled. "He's not yours either."

Laura just smiled, not smug, not cruel. Sad.

Like she knew something Monique didn't.

"I'm not here to be his anything," she repeated, softer now. "I'm here because your friend isn't the first woman to end up in hospital after being with him."

Those words slapped the breath from Monique's chest.

Monique stepped back automatically. "What are you talking about?"

Laura opened the door wider. "You'd better come in."

Monique hesitated. For the first time since meeting Laura, she felt something entirely new creeping up her spine, fear. Not of Laura, but of the truth she might be carrying.

Inside, the place was neat, clean, lived-in. Nothing of the girl Nate described, no abandoned wine glasses, no lingerie tossed on the floor, no perfume clouding the air. Nothing to suggest she had ever been there for pleasure.

"Sit," Laura said, nodding at the couch.

Monique obeyed, tense and coiled like she expected a knife in the back.

But Laura didn't attack.

She sat across from her, folded her hands, and spoke with a calm that made Monique's stomach twist.

"I'm not your competition," she said. "I'm not here to take him from you. I'm here for answers. Answers Nate will never give willingly."

Monique shook her head. "You don't understand him."

"What I understand," Laura cut in gently, "is that your friend Jane nearly died. And she's not the first."

Monique felt her chest squeeze, as if the room had shrunk around her. "How do you know anything about Jane?"

Laura exhaled slowly.

"Because I've been following Nate for months."

Silence dropped between them like a stone.

Monique's voice cracked. "Why?"

Laura's eyes flicked toward the window, watching the world outside as though something in it hurt.

When she looked back, her voice was softer. Colder. Older.

"Because my sister was one of his women. And she didn't survive him."

Monique's blood ran cold.

Laura lifted her hand before Monique could speak.

"No," she murmured. "Not yet. This story isn't for two people."

Monique swallowed. "What does that mean?"

"It means," Laura said, standing, "that you and I aren't enough. The three of us, you, me, and Jane, need to sit together. Because this isn't just seduction. It isn't jealousy. It isn't rivalry."

She stepped closer.

"It's danger."

Monique stared at her, heart pounding. When she finally found her voice, it barely held shape.

"Why the three of us?"

Passionate Poison

Laura didn't hesitate.

"Because we're the ones he targeted. Because we're the ones he thinks he can break. Because he doesn't expect us to talk to each other."

Then she leaned in, her voice a whisper of steel.

"And because we're going to destroy him."

***

Hours later, when Monique returned to my hospital room with Laura trailing behind her, I felt the shift instantly. Something electric. Heavy. Foreboding.

I could barely sit up, tubes in my arms, chest aching with every breath… but I forced myself upright.

Laura stepped into the low light of my room.

"Jane," she said quietly. "We need to talk. All three of us."

And that's when I knew:

Whatever truth she carried was going to change everything.

***

I hear their footsteps before I see them. Slow, hesitant, almost careful, as if the corridor itself knows something dreadful is about to happen. I push myself upright, even though the movement sends a wave of dizziness rolling through me. My chest feels tight, my hands tremble, and the monitor beside me gives off an irritated little beep that the nurse warned me about.

But then I see her.

Laura.

Walking in behind Monique with a calmness that feels rehearsed, like someone who's spent weeks pretending not to be afraid. She looks nothing like the girl Nate had spoken to in that soft, intimate voice. She isn't fragile. She isn't naïve. She isn't dazzled by him.

She's here with purpose.

Monique closes the door behind them, her shoulders tense. She sits beside me, taking my hand as if bracing for an impact neither of us can see yet. Laura moves to the foot of the bed, placing a thick, worn notebook on her lap. The edges are battered, dog-eared, weathered by grief and long nights.

"Jane," she says softly, "I'm sorry you're seeing me like this… and under these circumstances. But you need the truth. Both of you do."

Her voice is steady, but I hear something underneath, a hurt so deep it's almost audible.

I swallow, trying to ignore the dryness in my throat. "Then tell me. Whatever it is. I can take it."

She hesitates for only a second before flipping open her notebook. Pages covered in handwriting, newspaper clippings, printed emails, dates, times, medical reports. It looks like the inside of someone's mind when they're solving a crime.

"I'm an investigative journalist," she begins. "I've been working undercover for several months, following a lead that no one else wanted to touch. A series of deaths, women, all around Nate's age range, all romantically attached to him at some point."

My blood goes cold. I feel Monique stiffen beside me.

Laura turns the notebook toward us. A photo stares up at me, smiling face, bright eyes, young. Too young.

"Her name was Mia," Laura says, voice cracking. "My little sister."

My heart clenches. "I'm so sorry."

"She was twenty-four," Laura continues. "Smart. Funny. Strong. And then she met Nate." Her jaw tightens. "Within weeks she changed. She became anxious, paranoid, convinced she wasn't good enough for him… that she had to 'earn' his love."

The words slice right through me. It's every thought I've had for months.

Passionate Poison

Laura continues, flipping to the next page. Another face. And another. Ten in total.

Ten women who look terrifyingly like me and Monique, vibrant at first, then progressively hollow-eyed in the later photos Laura points out.

"All of them were ruled suicides," Laura says. "Each had a note. And every note said the same thing: *I wasn't enough for him. He deserves better. I can't live with disappointing him.*"

The room feels colder. The hospital blanket suddenly feels too thin.

"That sounds like... conditioning," Monique whispers. "Not love."

"It wasn't love," Laura says. "It was calculated. Methodical. And chemical."

My breath stops in my lungs.

Chemical.

I remember the drink with the bitter aftertaste. The dizziness. Losing time. The ache in my chest. The way my thoughts wrapped themselves around Nate like vines, tight, irrational, desperate.

"I found traces of a sedative, an obedience drug," Laura continues, lowering her voice. "Highly addictive. It makes the victim emotionally dependent on the person administering it. It breaks judgement, weakens resistance, alters perception of fear." Her eyes meet mine. "It also damages the heart."

I grip the blanket, knuckles white. My heart monitor spikes.

"So it wasn't just me," I whisper. "It wasn't that I was weak. Or stupid. It wasn't even love. It was... chemical." Tears burn my eyes. "He did this to me."

"To all of us," Monique murmurs, looking shaken. "He tried to give me a drink the night... the night we," She swallows hard. "But I didn't take it."

Laura nods. "That's why I came for you today, Monique. You were next. You and Jane. He doesn't keep women long. Not once they start asking questions or showing independence."

A long silence presses down on the room like a heavy blanket. I feel my chest tighten again, but not from illness, this time it's fury.

"How long have you been tracking him?" I ask.

"Months," Laura answers. "Mia's death didn't sit right with me. Neither did the police report. So I dug deeper. I found the pattern. I needed to get close to him to prove it."

"And you did," I whisper.

She nods. "He trusts easily when he thinks someone admires him. It was sickening, but necessary."

Monique wipes a tear. "Why didn't you tell me when we met?"

"Because you weren't ready to hear it," Laura says gently. "Jane wasn't either. And I needed you both alive."

Alive.

The word hits different now.

I look at the faces in the notebook one more time. Ten women whose names should never have been written inside a file of deaths. Ten women who believed they weren't enough. Ten women who lost themselves to a man who never saw them as people.

I lift my gaze to Laura and Monique, two women who could have easily been on that list.

Then to the door, where Nate could walk in at any moment.

The truth settles in my bones like ice.

"We need to stop him," I say quietly.

Laura nods.

"We will."

***

Passionate Poison

I sat there propped up against the cold metal rails of the hospital bed, my heartbeat flickering on the monitor like it couldn't decide whether to stay or go. Laura's words were still hanging in the air, thick and poisonous, sinking into my bones. Ten women. Ten lives that collapsed the same way mine almost had. Ten notes that all said the same damn thing.

Not good enough for him.

I felt the room tilt. Not from illness this time, but from the weight of realisation sliding into place like a blade finding the small gap between ribs.

"It wasn't love…" My voice cracked, barely more than a breath. "It was chemicals."

Laura nodded slowly, her expression softening in a way that told me she'd said those words herself once, alone, in the dark, grieving her sister. Monique sucked in a hard breath beside me, her knuckles white where she gripped the bedrail. She didn't look at me. She didn't need to. I could feel her guilt radiating off her, like heat from a cracked stove.

And for the first time, I didn't blame her.

Because this thing, this obsession, this madness, didn't come from us. It never did.

It came from him.

Laura flipped open her notebook again, showing us scribbled diagrams of behavioural changes, timelines, medical anomalies. "Every woman deteriorated the same way," she said quietly. "Confusion. Anxiety. Sleep disruption. Physical dependency. They all reported feeling… tethered to him. Like they couldn't leave."

Monique's voice was small. "I was starting to feel like that too."

I reached for her hand without thinking. She flinched, then let me take it, gripping back with a desperation I recognised because it lived inside me too. This wasn't the Monique who posed in my mirror, teasing and glamorous. This was the Monique who'd been lying next to a monster believing she was special.

Just like I had.

"Jane," Laura said gently, "you weren't imagining any of it. The paranoia. The mood swings. The way your body started shutting down." She swallowed hard. "My sister went through the exact same thing. By the end, she was convinced she couldn't breathe properly unless he was in the room."

My stomach twisted. I remembered nights with Nate where I'd clung to him without understanding why. I remembered thinking I was losing my mind. That I was needy. Pathetic. Weak.

But I wasn't.

I was drugged.

"He almost killed you," Monique whispered, tears forming in her eyes. "He would've killed you, Jane. You know that, right?"

The heart monitor beeped steadily, but my pulse thudded painfully under my skin.

I nodded. "Yeah. I know."

For the first time since I'd met her, Laura's strong, unshakeable voice wavered. "I can't let him do it again. To anyone. Not after my sister." She closed her notebook. "But I can't take him down alone. He's clever. He covers his tracks. And every woman who's died? No one questioned it. Not one detective, not one doctor, not one family member, except me."

Her eyes locked on mine with a sharp, electric determination. "But now there are three of us."

A strange thing happened then, something I didn't expect. The guilt, the heartbreak, the humiliation... it didn't vanish. But it shifted. Like the ground under me had stopped cracking and instead started forming something new. Something fierce.

A weapon.

Passionate Poison

"We need evidence," Laura continued. "Real evidence. Medical. Psychological. Physical. Patterns of behaviour. Digital traces. Women he's contacted. Women he's groomed. Financial transactions. Everything."

Monique exhaled shakily. "I can get into his office. And his phone. He trusts me." Her face twisted as she said it, the irony sharp enough to cut. "Or at least, he thinks he does."

I squeezed her hand. "That's exactly what we need."

"And Jane," Laura said softly, "you know things about him no one else does. Details. Routines. His temper. His habits. His weaknesses."

Weaknesses.

Funny word for a man who'd built himself up like he was untouchable.

I straightened a little, wincing at the ache in my chest. "He hurt me. He manipulated me. He drugged me. He made me think I was losing myself." I looked at both women. "But he's forgotten who I actually am."

Monique's eyes lit with something dangerous, something I'd seen in her only a few times before, when life had backed her into a corner. "So we take him down."

Laura nodded. "We stop him before he destroys anyone else."

A long silence followed, thick, heavy, deliberate. A vow forming in the air.

Then the footsteps came.

Slow. Confident. Familiar.

Nate.

His shadow stretched across the bottom of the door before his knuckles tapped lightly, politely, like he hadn't nearly killed me.

"Jane, baby doll? You awake?" His voice slid under the door like smoke.

The three of us looked at each other.

United.

Awake.

Changed.

I turned my head toward the nurse's station and said, steady as glass:

"Don't let him in."

The footsteps stopped.

For the first time since this nightmare began, the door stayed closed.

And I felt something inside me shift, something small, but powerful.

Control.

Chapter Ten:
Beyond Lust Lies Salvation

I never thought freedom would feel this fragile. Even once the doctors finally discharged me, heart steady, blood finally clear of whatever poison Nate had been slipping into my system, I still felt like one wrong step could send me spiralling again. But I wasn't the woman he'd broken anymore; I was the woman rebuilding herself, piece by bloody piece.

While I'd been stuck in a hospital bed, Laura and Monique had been doing the kind of work I physically couldn't: slipping themselves into Nate's orbit as if they'd never left, never suspected, never known. Watching them walk into the hospital on the day of my release, steady, composed, united, I knew the tide had turned.

They weren't puppets anymore.

They were bait.

And I was the one holding the wire.

***

Laura settles first, the innocent act perfected

Laura moved into the role almost too convincingly. She walked into Nate's life like a soft breeze: sweet voice, shy smiles, pretending to be flattered whenever he touched her arm or told her how "special" she was. She even giggled at his terrible jokes. The bastard had always loved an easy audience.

But beneath that softness, she was all blade.

Night after night, she sat with him while he rambled about business deals, his sexual "prowess," his bloody *importance*. She asked naive questions that let him brag without noticing what he was revealing. She let him think she was falling for him.

And in return, he loosened his tongue… and his habits.

Linine Langley

I'd warned her what the drug tasted like, that faint bitterness, sharp at the back of the throat. So every time he offered her a drink, she'd take the glass, tilt it to her lips just enough for him to believe, then slip it away when he wasn't looking.

Later, she'd spit it into a container for testing.

Every night, she fed us information.

Every night, Nate fed his ego.

He thought she worshipped him.

He thought she was his next masterpiece.

He had no idea she was documenting his downfall in real time.

***

And Monique… God. Watching her step back into his arms so effortlessly made me realise just how good she was at playing whatever part the world needed her to.

She flirted lightly, laughed too loudly, touched his shoulder like she missed him. She apologised for "misunderstanding him" and acted guilty for "hurting me." She made herself seem small, sorry, eager to please, exactly the type of woman he believed she'd always been.

But I knew better.

Monique had turned her guilt into purpose.

Her softness was now a weapon.

Her job wasn't to seduce him.

It was to distract him, from Laura, from me, from the cameras soon hidden in every corner of his home.

And he fell for it.

Hook, line, bloody sinker.

***

Two months later, I return

Passionate Poison

When I walked back into Nate's house for the first time after hospital, my chest tightened, not with fear, but with clarity. The rooms weren't haunted anymore. They were crime scenes waiting to be captured.

Laura and Monique hugged me at the door, both whispering the same thing into my ear:

"He doesn't suspect a thing."

Our plan clicked into place that very night.

Tiny cameras, in light fixtures, behind books, inside vents, embedded in decorative frames. Impossible to see unless you knew where they were.

We didn't need to manipulate him.

We just needed to let him be himself.

***

We took turns with him like actors in a rotating play.

Laura presented innocence, all wide eyes and soft questions. She let him think he was shaping her, moulding her, creating another obedient doll.

Monique presented devotion, the kind he thought he deserved. She left just enough jealousy in the air to stroke his ego, just enough flirtation to make him forget she'd ever betrayed him.

And I presented forgiveness.

That was the hardest role of my life.

Sitting beside him.

Letting him touch me.

Letting him believe he still had power over me.

Each time he brushed my cheek or pressed a kiss to my shoulder, I felt that old panic spark at the base of my spine. But I breathed through it. I reminded myself:

You're not his prey anymore.

Linine Langley

You're here to burn him down.

***

And Nate? He couldn't help himself.

The first night all three of us were there, he poured drinks like a host entertaining guest. Whiskey for him. Moscato for Laura. A red for Monique. A sparkling water for me, the one he thought I'd never suspect.

He talked big, business, sex, power, while his hand slid the smallest pill into the water bottle, he handed me.

He did it again the next week.

And the next.

And the next.

Each time, every camera caught him clean.

His fingers.

The pill.

The dissolve.

The hand-off.

Stamped in cold, digital clarity.

Four weeks of footage.

Four weeks of chemical proof.

Four weeks of him damning himself with his own arrogance.

He thought lust made us blind.

He thought control made us loyal.

He thought he was the hunter.

He had no idea he was already in the trap.

***

Passionate Poison

For weeks it felt like living inside a long, held breath. Every night we choreographed our lies so carefully they began to feel like truths. Laura was the ingénue who never stopped smiling; Monique was the penitent lover with a ready shoulder; I was the forgiving wife, the woman who laughed and slid into his arms as if everything was as it had always been. All the while, little black boxes recorded him, the clink of spoons, the tilt of a bottle, the precise, practiced way he measured powders into glasses.

Watching the footage back, frame by frame, was the closest thing to proof I'd ever seen. There was Nate mixing things into the youngest woman's drink with the same faintly arrogant smile he used on me. There was him leaning in, whispering that rehearsed line about belonging, about how they were special. There were images of him treating each girl like a prize he'd already labelled and shelved. He seemed unstoppable in his arrogance, convinced the world bowed to him.

We kept our routine tight. We never overlapped too much. Our appointments around him were small and careful, a text here, a laugh there. We never showed the cameras each other. We never let our faces reveal more than the precise emotion the camera needed to see. It felt like war, slow, surgical, exhausting.

And like all wars, there were moments when the enemy smelled fear and grew dangerous.

Nate was getting restless. We could see it in the footage and feel it in the house. He started watching Laura more, not in the way he watched me, possessive and possessory, but like a hunter watching the one rabbit that might outrun him. Monique noticed his ways of testing her, his little insinuations. He would make a joke that cut close and see if she flinched. He would move an inch too near and watch for her reaction. He liked to prod the edges of control and see who pulled back.

That night felt like a slow exhale that went wrong.

We were in the study, dim light, two laptops open, breath held together with a playlist of white noise in the background so the house wouldn't sense the quiet. Monique and I were cross-referencing timestamps, matching the times Nate left the room with the moments a woman began to behave oddly. We were building a chain: glass, powder, slump, confusion.

"Look at this," Monique whispered, pointing. "Three different girls, same movement of his hand. Same pause. Same look."

I watched, heart thudding. He had a rhythm, like a metronome that made sense only when you could see it over and over.

We watched more footage, and then Laura's face filled the laptop screen. She was sitting on the sofa, a cardigan round her shoulders, smile careful. Nate was across from her, relaxed, the kind of proud and lazy that comes before someone decides they're untouchable. He was mid-sentence about something trivial when Laura said, with that soft, impossible voice of hers,

"You used to know my sister, didn't you?"

The room on the screen froze, and in the pause, I felt the air shift. Nate's face changed in a way I'd never seen on camera. The studied ease fell away like a mask. Something hard and quick passed through his expression and I felt it like an electric shock. He blinked, recalibrated, then smiled a fraction too slow. The mask slid back on, but the tremor was there.

"Did she?" Nate asked, the words measured, like he was catching his breath.

I swallowed and leaned closer. My knuckles were white on the desk.

Monique's whisper was a razor: "That wasn't an accident."

We should have known then that the moment would come. Predators smell the first scent of danger and test. We watched the rest of the night unfold like a slow-motion collision. On the feed, Nate stood and moved toward Laura. He spoke softly; she answered. He got close.

Passionate Poison

Too close. His hand was at her throat for a blink, a movement that made my stomach drop so low I thought I'd be sick.

Monique and I didn't need a second to decide. We snatched our jackets; we didn't stop to argue. The house was maddeningly quiet when we left the study, a silence that felt intentionally held.

As we hurried down the hallway, the cameras still rolling, my mind ran a dozen frantic equations. Did we leave a gap in our plan? Had we been too confident? Had Nate finally worked out the shape of our trap? My mouth tasted of metal and adrenaline.

I heard the first sound before I saw it, a strangled, sharp intake, a noise that hadn't belonged to laughter or lovemaking. It was a human sound, terrified and small.

We burst into the living room at the same time. Through the doorway I saw them: Laura backed against the bookcase, one hand up at her throat, her face white, her lips forming something she couldn't finish. Nate was there, not the gentleman from dinner, not the quiet, watchful man who'd charmed me into submission, but a version with a quick, terrible edge in his eyes. His hand was tight at her throat, his other arm braced against the wood as if holding himself steady.

For a fraction of a second everything slowed. The camera in the corner of the room kept whirring, innocent and blunt, recording a crime the way an automaton might.

I saw red then, not in a cinematic way, but the flaring, hot focus that closes down everything else. Monique shoved past me, a fierce animal, and I followed. I don't remember how we reached them, only that the instinct to protect shoved aside every other thought. My voice felt enormous and raw when I screamed.

Nate's head snapped toward us. For the first time since we began this plan, his eyes were unguarded. There was hatred there, quick, bright, dangerous.

Linine Langley

He let go like a man dropping a thing that's burned him. Laura slid to the floor, gasping, and Nate took a step back as if he'd been surprised by his own hands.

For a long heartbeat no one spoke. The recorded footage kept rolling, pitiless. Outside, the night was quiet in the way a thing holds its breath when something has gone very wrong.

We were close, closer than we'd ever been to being found, to being unmasked. The evidence existed on hard drives and cameras, but it had become urgent in a way the footage couldn't capture: a woman on the floor, a predator who'd shown his claws.

"Phone 000," Monique said, voice brittle. "Now."

My hands shook as I dialled. The tiny whirr of the line connected felt enormous. I watched Nate's face tighten. He looked like a man who had been caught in a mirror and hated the view.

The minutes thudded. The cameras kept their unblinking record. What we had spent months building was suddenly a fragile thing, evidence, yes, but also the immediate rush of survival. We'd planned for subtlety and patience. We hadn't planned for his lash.

As I crouched beside Laura and tried to make her breathe, I felt the truth settle heavy and absolute. He wasn't just arrogant. He was dangerous. And the footage we'd collected was no longer proof for a courtroom, it was a lifeline for a woman gasping on the carpet.

Outside, sirens began to cut through the night.

***

I never hear Laura scream.

What I hear instead is silence, the kind that drops into a room like a stone into deep black water. A silence so sharp it slices through walls.

Monique and I freeze.

Something is wrong.

Passionate Poison

Wrong in the way the air goes still before a storm. Wrong in the way predators stop moving when they realise the hunt is over.

Then I hear Nate's voice, low, strained, struggling to stay calm.

"Laura... what exactly did you mean by that?"

My blood runs cold.

Monique and I don't look at each other. We just move.

When we turn the corner into the hallway, we see it, not violence, not yet, but something far more terrifying: Nate's mask is gone.

His posture is rigid, one arm outstretched, caging Laura against the wall.

His expression carved from ice.

His eyes... black with recognition.

And Laura, clever, brave Laura, stands perfectly still, refusing to flinch, like she's staring down a wild animal and knows that running is how you get mauled.

Nate senses us before he sees us. His body snaps tight, shoulders lifting, jaw clenching hard enough to crack bone. When he turns around, the smile he forces is something monstrous, stretched, wrong, a parody of charm.

"There you are," he says softly. Too softly. "All of us together. Isn't that nice."

My skin prickles. My pulse thunders. Every instinct whisper:

We're seconds from disaster.

But before he can speak again, before he can corner Laura properly, before the façade can repair itself, sirens wail in the distance.

Faint, but unmistakable.

Nate hears them too.

His eyes flick, only for a breath, but it's enough.

Linine Langley

Laura straightens. Monique steps forward.

And I, still trembling, still recovering, still learning to breathe without chemicals in my bloodstream, lift my phone so he can see the screen.

"They'll be here any minute."

The look on his face cracks.

Not fear.

Not anger.

Something deeper. A god realising the temple he built is finally collapsing.

He laughs once, a harsh, unbelieving exhale.

"You think you've won?"

His voice is steady, controlled, terrifyingly calm.

"You have no idea what you've started."

But he's wrong.

Because for the first time since I met him, *I do know*.

I know exactly what he is.

Exactly what he's done.

Exactly who he's hurt.

And I know what we are now, too: Three women who walked through hell and came back carrying fire.

The sirens get louder.

Tyres screech outside.

Doors slam.

Boots thunder up the path.

Nate takes one step back, only one, and looks at me like I'm something he can still own, still break, still mould.

But I don't look away.

Passionate Poison

Not anymore.

"You can't control us," I whisper.

My voice doesn't shake.

"My mind… my heart… my life… none of it belongs to you now."

For the first time ever, *he flinches*.

And that's when the police burst in.

Officers flood the hallway, shouting commands. Nate lifts his hands slowly, still smiling, still pretending he's untouchable, but his eyes betray him. The confidence isn't real anymore.

He's arrested. Restrained. Taken away.

He doesn't fight. He doesn't plead.

He watches me as he's led out the door, a silent promise of resentment burning in his gaze.

But for once… he's the one locked out.

He's the one losing control.

He's the one who finally sees the truth:

his empire was built on women who have now risen against him.

When the door closes behind him, the three of us stand motionless in the shattered quiet.

Laura exhales shakily.

Monique wipes her eyes.

And I feel something strange wash through me.

Not victory.

Not relief.

Not safety.

Something purer.

Something older.

Linine Langley

Something earned through fire:

Freedom.

Epilogue: The End of a Reign

I never thought I'd see the day Nate Hawthorne stood behind bars, stripped of every mask he'd ever worn. But life has a strange way of forcing truth into the light, even when it's buried beneath charm, power, and beautifully-crafted lies.

The trial was brutal, months of evidence, testimonies, psychological reports, and the quiet bravery of women who thought they'd never speak again. I watched them file into the courtroom one by one, shoulders trembling but heads held high. Survivors. Just like me.

When the sentence was handed down, the room didn't cheer. It exhaled.

Life imprisonment.

And the new legislation, the one passed in the wake of rising violence against women, sealed the rest. Castration for offenders found guilty of sexual assault while their victims were incapacitated. Nate's face didn't move when the judge read that part. But his eyes did. For the first time since I'd known him, he looked… small.

I attended his intake hearing at the prison. Not out of loyalty. Not revenge. Closure. He was led out in chains, no designer suit, no cologne, no smirk. Just a man stripped of the only weapon he'd ever valued.

He met my gaze only once. A flicker, confusion, anger, something like disbelief. As if he couldn't comprehend that three women, he thought he owned had brought him down.

I didn't look away.

Monique was beside me, fierce as ever. Laura, steady and unbroken, stood on my other side. We were silent. United. Free.

Nate disappeared through a steel door that clanged shut behind him.

Linine Langley

And with that sound, sharp, final, the spell broke. The danger, the chaos, the poison of him… gone.

What remains now is ours: our lives, our strength, our future.

We survived him.

And that is the truest justice of all.

www.ingramcontent.com/pod-product-compliance
Lightning Source LLC
Chambersburg PA
CBHW052055070526
44584CB00017B/2194